A HISTORY OF
THE MERCHANTS HOUSE
OF GLASGOW

by J. M. REID

IN THE BEGINNING . . .

This relief showing three early Merchants (possibly pensioners) is the
oldest possession of the Merchants House

PREFACE

There is a history in all men's lives,
Figuring the nature of the times deceas'd,
The which observ'd, a man may prophesy,
With a near aim, of the main chance of things
As yet not come to life; which in their seeds
and weak beginnings lie intreasured.

So Shakespeare wrote nearly four hundred years ago and centuries before that mediaeval merchants were beginning to organise themselves for the purpose of trade, for the care of those amongst them whom ill fortune had overwhelmed, and for the good government of the towns in which they dwelt. This happened in Glasgow as in other places, and I am sure that few will read The History of the Merchants House, which Mr. J. M. Reid has so graphically written, without feeling, even in these present days, part of a long tradition—a tradition in which the claims of business and trade were blended with a wider outlook of service and community responsibility.

The Merchants House is still concerned with affairs arising from these original concepts; and, although in the course of long years the emphasis has altered from one aspect to another, it continues to bear an important position in the affairs of the great city which Glasgow has become. Both directly and indirectly, the members take their part in various sides of Civic responsibility, and in particular the House is deeply concerned with men and women who have fallen upon unfortunate and difficult times. In the Chapter headed " The Age of Bequests " and in other places in the book, Mr. Reid has described some of the gifts large and small which have been given to the House by citizens of the past and the present for schemes of benevolence and education, and it is good to think of the men of long ago and those of more recent times being somehow or other linked together in the furtherance of a common purpose. The Skippers and Mariners belonging to the Burgh who in 1687 contributed to the funds of the House " for behoof of poor and decayed Merchants and Mariners the sum of eightpence in the pund Scots of their wages " were surely in the same tradition as the great Inverclyde Bequest for Seamen set up over three hundred years later and administered by the Merchants House of today.

The Deans of Guild and their Councils of these present times are no longer required to follow the terms of the Act by the Scots Parliament of 1593 and be " men chosen and appointed . . . to judge and decerne in all actiones concerning merchandis "; but the Merchants House still elects the Dean of Guild who constitutes the Dean of Guild Court, aided by four Lyners elected by the Merchants House and four Lyners elected by the Trades House and who in the words of the Letter of Guildry of 1605 is still responsible in Glasgow for deciding " on all questions of neighbourhood and lyning " that is of building and the laying out of streets.

It is a fascinating account of community interest and care reaching back into the mists of history, and which is still alive and vital today. The grateful thanks of all the Members of the House are due both to Mr. J. M. Reid for his exact and vivid story and also to the enthusiasm and interest of the Members of the Sub-Committee under the Chairmanship of Sir John S. Muirhead, who throughout have been concerned with the project. It is just over a century since the publication of Dr. W. H. Hill's massive VIEW OF THE MERCHANTS HOUSE OF GLASGOW and this book brings the history of the House up to our own day in an easily readable form. Finally, it is of interest to note that under the Will of the late Dr. James A. McCallum, Collector and Clerk of the House from 1912 until 1948, part of the expense of the present History comes from a gift which long ago he provided for the purpose.

THOMAS G. ROBINSON,
Dean of Guild

CONTENTS

ILLUSTRATIONS

CHAPTER I

BEGINNINGS

THERE have been merchants in Glasgow ever since it became a burgh. This is surely the meaning of the Charter granted by King William the Lyon in or soon after the year 1175, which declares that its burgesses "shall have my firm peace throughout all my land in going and returning"—evidently in the course of trade. The town itself was to enjoy "all the liberties and customary rights that any of my burghs possess".

These were important privileges. Glasgow was, of course, a very old place even eight hundred years ago, but it was a very small one, known only for its church which had become the seat of a bishopric, stretching from Loch Lomond to the Border. For Scotland in those days organised towns were something new. Kings were founding them where markets and fairs could be held under the protection of castles. There merchants and craftsmen could gather safely. They could deal with their own problems and settle their disputes in courts held under the guidance of the king's representatives, called bailies, aldermen or provosts.

This was a kind of life not known till then. Everywhere outside the little burghs, affairs were managed by feudal lords or chiefs, or by the king's sheriffs, most of whom were lords themselves. The new burghs were the germs of self-governing communities. They were given the right to be the only centres of trade in wide districts. Custom duties were paid on the goods sold in their market places, and this revenue went to the Crown.

Most of the new burghs were built on land which belonged to the king. Their people were the king's tenants, just as the feudal lords were, though the patches of ground on which they built their houses—and raised most of their own food—were tiny. But in this Glasgow was exceptional. Its land belonged to the Bishop. The castle which protected it was the Bishop's. Its burgesses were the Bishop's men. Not trade but the affairs of the Church—including the Bishop's important law courts—gave it its chief business. Yet its merchants were granted the same rights as those of the Royal Burghs. When Rutherglen, Renfrew, and Dumbarton, all of them King's Burghs, tried to interfere with Glasgow's trading or to raise tolls on the goods brought to its market, they were forbidden to do this, though quarrels with them over Glasgow's trading rights persisted for centuries.

All the same, King James VI was not so very far wrong when he declared that Glasgow was "at the beginning one very mean and simple town without ather trafficke or nowmer of inhabitants". When the burgh was new it had perhaps 1500 people; though it had become a university city and the ecclesiastical capital of the west, under an archbishop after 1491, it does not seem to have had much more than 4500 before the Reformation. No doubt because of this and because the Cathedral was still more important than the city its institutions appear to have developed more slowly than those of some other Scots burghs.

Even in the thirteenth century merchant guilds seem to have existed in some Scottish towns. This was natural, since guilds were common in England and other parts of Europe. They were associations of burgesses whose members paid something to belong to them. "Guild" is very much the same word as "gold"; in the Glasgow Merchants' House the record of membership was to be called "The Gold Book".

The guilds served many different purposes. They were friendly associations which helped members and their families when they fell into difficulties, as the Merchants' House does still. They organised special religious services for themselves. It was their function to protect the business interests of merchants or particular groups of craftsmen, but a "gildrie" could also become the body responsible for effective local government in a town, electing councillors perhaps provosts and bailies when these became officials of the burgh and not of the king or ecclesiastical lord. Many mediaeval cities were, in fact, ruled by their guilds; in others the guildry seems to have been little more than another name for the whole effective body of burgesses, the "community". In Scottish towns the Dean of Guild, normally the head of the merchants, was sometimes elected by the Town Council; there might indeed be a Dean without any guild.

If more of Glasgow's records had survived we might have a clearer idea of the Merchant Guild's first beginnings here. In the bigger Scottish burghs control of the towns' affairs seems to have tended to fall into the hands of the merchants during the later Middle Ages when "head courts" that could be attended by all the burgesses became less important and new councillors and bailies came to be chosen by the existing ones and not by the citizens.

Though merchants may sometimes have been little more than shopkeepers they were usually the richest burgesses and the most important to royal governments which looked for taxes from the towns.

Partly in reaction against this state of things craftsmen began to organise themselves into separate guilds for each occupation whose heads, called "deacons" claimed the right to act with the town councillors. These were the Incorporated Trades. In Glasgow it was not till 1516 that the first of them, the Skinners, was granted a charter or "seal of cause" by the Town Council. As new guilds were organised no artizan was allowed to practise his craft unless he belonged to the appropriate body. Though Glasgow's foreign commerce was growing—particularly in salmon and herring from the Clyde—there was still no official merchant guild, but the merchants were drawing together. By 1569 they had a voluntary association with a President and funds of its own. For taxation purposes they had already been recognised as a group distinct from the craftsmen. They had perhaps already built themselves a hospital for the care of their poor and as a meeting place for themselves. In 1582 their President, George Elphinstone, asked for an official writ of incorporation. This was not granted, but one may say that at this date Glasgow's Merchant Guild was at last ready to be born.

The Reformation might have killed the little city of the archbishops, which had depended so much on the power and wealth of the Roman Church. But, in fact, Glasgow "beautifully placed and pleasant, abounding with garden stuff, apple trees and orchards", according to Bishop Leslie, soon began to grow fast. It had, perhaps, 7000 people by the end of the century. From its market fat cattle, wool and skins, butter and cheese went to the East Country, corn to the Western Lowlands, French wine, ale and aqua-vitae (presumably whisky) to Argyll and the Isles.

The merchants were sending out little ships from the Potterig, a roadstead on the Clyde above the future Port Glasgow. Glasgow merchants and their affairs were beginning to be of interest not only to themselves but to Scotland generally.

The Merchant House was indeed brought to birth not so much by the pressure of the Glasgow merchants themselves as by a general Scottish view of the proper shape of town government. Rivalry between craftsmen and merchants had led to long disputes, even riots, in many burghs. There seems to have been little trouble of this sort in Glasgow apart from one incident in 1583 when a craftsman tried to insist on ranking himself with the merchants at a wapinschaw, the parade of burgesses equipped with arms to keep order in the city or defend it. But in Edinburgh the young King James VI himself found that he must head a court of arbitration between craftsmen and merchants which worked out a new constitution for his capital city. An Act of the Scottish Parliament in 1593 laid it down that in all burghs a Dean of Guild and his Council should be established on the Edinburgh pattern "to judge and declare on all actions covering merchandise . . . . . . according to the lovable form of jugement as it is in all good tounis of France and Flanderis," especially Paris, Rouen, Bordeaux and La Rochelle. Two years later the Convention of Royal Burghs followed this up with a letter to the Provost, Bailies and Council of Glasgow declaring that its members were "nocht a little offendit that thai [the Glasgow Magistrates and Councillors] conform nocht themsellfes to the comlie ordour of other fre burrowis in haifing ane deyne of gild and electing gild brether". The Convention was a powerful body, a sort of supplementary parliament for the Third Estate of the national Parliament in which all royal burghs had a right to be represented. Glasgow was not yet a royal burgh, but because of its importance it already sent commissioners to both Parliament and the Convention. A merchant and a craft deacon were specially delegated to discuss the Convention's message at its next meeting.

A proposal of this sort, said the Glasgow men, was a novelty for their town. It might cause disputes. They hoped the Convention would not press it. The Convention sent them home with a copy of the Edinburgh form of Guildry, which their town council, merchants and craftsmen were asked to consider. Glasgow still refused to be hustled, even though the proposed change was backed by the Convention, Parliament and the King himself. The Convention had to raise the matter more than once again. It was not till November 8th, 1604, that "the whole body of the Merchant Rank" present in the city, and the deacons of the crafts met, separately, to appoint commissioners to discuss the ending of controversies between Merchants and Craftsmen and the election of a Dean of Guild and his Council. Two days later the commissioners actually came together—eleven from the Merchants (including two bailies) and thirteen from the crafts (with one bailie). They, in turn, appointed oversmen or arbiters to draw up a final agreement. It is interesting to note that only eight of those present, seven of them Merchants, were able to sign their own names.

At last, on February 6th, 1605, the oversmen—Sir George Elphinstone, Provost of Glasgow, and the three city ministers, David Weemis, John Bell and Robert Scott—with the agreement of the commissioners, produced the Letter of Guildry which still forms the basic constitution of the Glasgow Merchants' House and Trades House and, indeed, fixed the form of local government in the city itself for more than three hundred years. In our day, when every important change in town affairs has to be made under Parliamentary authority and the guidance of Government Departments it is worth remembering that, in spite of the pressure of the Convention of Royal Burghs, this long-lasting reform was finally worked out and enforced solely by Glasgow people themselves. As soon as it had been approved by the Town Council it came into force. Certainly it was confirmed by an Act of the Scots Parliament in 1672, but by that time it had been working for half a century, bringing (says the Act) "great peace, unitie and concord amongst themselves" to the inhabitants of Glasgow. With the Letter of Guildry the history of the Merchants' House had fully begun.

CHAPTER II

THE LETTER OF GUILDRY

WE can learn a good deal about the life and business of Glasgow in 1605, as well as about its institutions, from the Letter of Guildry. For instance, substantial citizens (or their wives and servants) brew their own beer and bake their own bread—probably in the form of oat or barley bannocks. They may salt beef, herring and salmon for their own use and even make their own candles. Of course they can buy all these things in shops or the town's market if they choose. Butter, eggs, fresh herring, pears, apples, onions, kail and milk are so common that to sell them is "not agreeable to the honour of the calling of a guild brother"—that is, of the superior class of citizen, merchant or craftsman, who might hope to have something to do with the management of the town's affairs.

Home grown foods and things made in Scotland were not all that a Glasgow man might enjoy more than three and a half centuries ago. He could buy wine, spices, sugars, "confections, wet or dry", drugs, silks, lawn, taffetas or hats from France, Flanders, England, or other foreign parts. Only guild brothers, however, were to be allowed to sell these things or deal in the products which were the Glasgow merchant's chief exports—plaiding, superior woollen or linen cloth (and the dyes and yarns that went to the making of cloth); salt fish and meat wholesale; sheepskins, hides, and the skins of wild animals (particularly foxes and otters); or tallow wholesale.

Craftsmen sold their own work, usually made to the customer's order, but it does not appear that, cloth and cured skins apart, much of their produce found its way into trade outside Glasgow and the neighbourhood. The little city had its merchants, but manufacturers were only beginning to have a place in its trade.

Though the Letter of Guildry lays the legal foundation of both the Merchants' House and the Trades House it mentions neither of them by name. It refers repeatedly to the Merchant Rank and the Craftsman Rank as things already recognised and existing, and also to "both the estates of the said Merchants and Craftsmen"—within the burgh these are evidently "estates" in the same sense as the Three Estates of peers, barons and burgesses which made up the Parliament of Scotland. But the framers of this document set out to establish something different, something new for Glasgow. This was the Guildry, from which the Letter has taken its name.

In 1605 Glasgow was trying to organise itself according to the best municipal models, at home and abroad. For men of the time this meant finding a place for each of the inhabitants and putting and keeping him firmly in that place. We have seen something of the same kind, though on a bigger scale in our century, when the competitive rough-and-tumble of Victorian times has given way to a state of things where there is an appropriate trade union for every wage-earner, an official society or college or council for each grade of every profession, and trade associations for all employers and businessmen.

In our industrial society there were employers' associations and trade unions long before everyone concerned was expected to belong to one of them, or at least to be guided by the rules and agreements which they made. Similarly craft guilds and a mer-chants' association had been growing for a long time in Glasgow before they were brought formally into the fabric of the town's life.

From its beginnings as a burgh there had been two classes among the inhabitants, as there were in other towns. These were burgesses and unfreemen. To begin with the burgesses were men who held "tofts" of burgh land and paid dues for this to the bishop —as in a royal burgh they would have paid them to the king. They shared the burden of "watch and ward", which meant that they policed the town and defended it, and met in the Head Courts to nominate officials, make regulations and see justice done. They alone shared the privileges of regular trade and craftsmanship. The unfreemen were their servants or casual workers—to begin with they had been actual serfs who could be bought and sold with the land—or incomers who had not established themselves properly in the town.

As the city grew there was not enough land for all the burgesses. Men qualified themselves for this rank by buying the freedom of the burgh; and, though they still bore the burdens of taxation and watch and ward the burgesses no longer gathered to decide on the town's affairs in the Head Court—perhaps because there were too many of them. A council ruled the city, choosing candidates from among whom the archbishop or his representative named the provost and bailies. The council's members were chosen by the bailies, ex-bailies, councillors and ex-councillors in a complicated way. Of the three bailies two, as we have seen, were Merchants and one a Craftsman. The provost was always a Merchant, and the whole council consisted of Merchant or Craft burgesses.

But in 1605 it seemed necessary to tighten up this system still further. Aparently there were too many burgesses. Some did not live in Glasgow. Others were not "bearing burden" in the old way. There were among them "infamous and debauched men of evil life and conversation". One feels that the people so described may have included those who did not obey the town's regulations for trade and craft work and possibly hankered after rather more freedom than the authorities were prepared to allow them.

Such citizens were now to be excluded from most of the privileges of burgesship by the creation of the Guildry. Its head was to be a new official, the Dean of Guild, who would have a council of his own consisting of four Merchants and four Craftsmen. Every Dean was to be a Merchant, a merchant sailor and merchant venturer (that is to say, an overseas trader). He would be a town councillor *ex officio*. A Dean would be elected every year (though it was evidently assumed that he would normally hold office for two years running) by the provost, bailies and town council, re-inforced by the deacons of the Craft Guilds and a sufficient number of Merchants to make the two ranks equal at the election, from a list of three names proposed by the retiring Dean with the advice of 24 Merchants. Thus he would, in effect, be the leader of the Merchants in particular. He could call all the Merchants together for the ordering of their hospital and other necessary affairs.

It is in these provisions of the Letter of Guildry that the Merchants' House begins to take shape. The hospital, both a meeting place and the centre of assistance for merchants and their women and children who had fallen on evil days, was the material "house" itself, and the Dean's 24 advisers were the predecessors of the Merchants' House Directors of later times.

The Craftsmen were also to have a new head, again a town councillor *ex officio*—the Deacon Convener of the Trades. They were to have their own council of deacons and "assisters" and their hospital, the future Trades House.

But it should be noted that, unlike the Deacon Convener, the Dean of Guild was in effect, a magistrate of the town. Next in rank to the Provost, he was later to be known as the Lord Dean. His council of eight lyners, half merchants, half craftsmen was evidently intended to be the executive of the new Guildry. It could make regulations—"laws and statutes, heads and articles to be observed for the weel of the town"—though these must be approved by the town council.

The Dean and Council were evidently to control entry to the Guildry. It was provided, indeed, that every existing burgess actually living in the town and not "infamous and debauched", could become a guild brother on paying the nominal fees of one merk (3/4d. Scots*) to the Dean and 40d. to "the hospital of his calling"—this last condition meant that he must choose to be ranked as either a Merchant or a Craftsman. Even the "infamous and debauched" were to be allowed to continue their work in the town under supervision and their sons, if they were found worthy and able, were to have the same rights to follow their fathers' trade and become guild brethren as those of other burgesses.

Future candidates for the Guildry were to be more severely tested, however. A guild brother's lawful son could be admitted if he paid 20/- to the Dean of Guild and 5/- to the Merchants or Trades Hospital, but he must also have property of 500 merks if a merchant or 250 if a craftsman. A guild brother's daughter who married a burgess could have him admitted to the guildry at the same rate. This, the Letter of Guildry points out, was an inducement to apprentices who had served their time and become burgesses to marry their master's daughters; otherwise they might have to wait longer for membership of the Guildry and to pay £30, with 13/4 to their hospital.

The Dean of Guild and his council were also to have power to tax guild brethren not more than £100 in all at one time "for the welfare and maintainance of the estate and help of their decayed gildbrether, their wifes children and servants".

The Council could fix fines and penalties, for it was also a law court. It could punish unfreemen "using the liberty of a freeman within the burgh" by trading as Merchants or practicing crafts. It could judge "in all actions betwixt Merchant and Merchant and Merchant and Mariner and other guild brether in all matters of merchandise and other sic-like causes". It was to oversee weights and measures. With an existing town official, the Master of Work, it was to decide "on all questions of neighbourhood and lyning"— that is of building and the laying out of streets. This is the function which the Dean of Guild and his lyners (in Latin *limitatores*)

---

*One shilling Scots was the equivalent of a penny sterling. It should be remembered, however, that a penny sterling in 1605 was worth a good deal more than a shilling in the 1960s.

have retained throughout three and a half centuries. The Council
of 1605 is now the Dean of Guild Court. One rather surprising
rule laid down by the Letter of Guildry—that lawyers should never
practice in this court—was soon abandoned.

The entry money of Guild brothers and part of the fines im-
posed by the Dean of Guild's council was to be divided between
the Merchant Hospital and the Trades Hospital for the use of
decayed merchants or craftsmen or for "any good and Godly work
which may tend to the advancement of the common weill of this
toun". The Merchant's share was to be distributed by the Dean
of Guild with the advice of the Merchant Council—presumably
the four Merchant lyners—"and such others of the Merchant Rank
as he shall choose to that effect".

The picture of municipal Glasgow which the Letter of Guildry
gives us is a curiously complicated one to our eyes. There are still
unfreemen who have no rights as citizens and simple freemen
burgesses who may trade in a small way or work as journeymen in
the crafts but whose privileges as citizens are very limited indeed.
Above these stand the brethren of the Guildry, strictly divided
between Merchants and members of the Craft guilds—the Incorporated Trades. Only they can be wholesale traders or act inde-
pendently as artizans and makers of goods for sale. They have the
power to regulate their own work, and, through the Dean of Guild's
Council, to judge disputes among themselves and prosecute out-
siders who try to share their privileges. They do not actually choose
the town council, but it is, in fact, made up of guild-brethren—an
equal number of merchants and craftsmen according to a ruling of
King James VI in 1606—and the burgh Treasurer cannot spend more
than £10 without the consent of the Dean of Guild and Deacon
Convener. They provide a sort of social security for themselves and
their families which other citizens do not share, but they are also
expected to spend part of their joint funds for the good of the town
in general.

City government, Guildry, the general community of burgesses,
the two ranks of Merchants and Craftsmen are sometimes mixed
up together in what seems a confusing way. Even the Dean of
Guild, though at once head of the Guildry in general and chief of
the Merchants in particular, is actually named by the Town Council,
specially reinforced for this purpose. But, in fact, under the Letter
of Guildry every mature Glaswegian is duly ranked and knows
precisely where he stands in the little city's society—and where he

THE OLD MERCHANTS HALL

in the Briggate, as reconstructed in and after 1659. From *View of the Merchants House of Glasgow*, 1866

is expected to remain for the rest of his life. For a city already beginning to boil with commercial enterprise which was to grow stronger with each generation through the following centuries this may seem a remarkably rigid framework, but Glasgow had, in fact, equipped itself with the pattern of town life which was felt to be necessary almost everywhere in Europe in that day.

The Merchants' House itself, though not yet named, had come properly into being. It had its head, the Dean of Guild. It was soon to borrow its chief permanent official, the Collector, from the Dean's Council, of which the first Collectors were members chosen to gather fines and the entry money of Merchants. It was already beginning to receive bequests for the good of its members and their families in distress. The work of safeguarding the interests and relieving the distresses of businessmen and their families, which has usually been its first concern through the centuries, had made a full beginning.

B

CHAPTER III

THE FIRST HUNDRED YEARS

WE can still see three of the old Glasgow Merchants "in their habit as they lived" carved in relief on a freestone slab which came from the first Merchants' Hospital and is in the Merchants' Hall building of today. Two of them are wrapped in voluminous cloaks, wear high hats and have long staffs in their hands. A third, clerkly, figure with a skull cap stands in the background. All are heavily bearded.

Glasgow's first historian, John McUre (alias Campbell) suggested in the eighteenth century that they might represent early pensioners of the House—possibly because beards were out of fashion in his day and suggested to his mind old age and poverty. In fact the three have all the look of solid, prosperous citizens: there is nothing about them to indicate poverty. The faces are obviously portraits. Just conceivably they may stand for the first Dean of Guild, Matthew Trumble (Turnbull in today's spelling); Archibald Faulis, the first Collector, who succeeded him as Dean of Guild, and Archibald Heigait, Town Clerk of Glasgow, who was the first Clerk of the Dean of Guild's Council.

Near them is another relief showing a ship, three masted and high pooped, a symbol of the future of Glasgow and a reminder that all the early Deans were overseas traders.

To begin with the Dean of Guild and his Council had to assert themselves firmly. They were something new in the little city and (as always) there were citizens suspicious of novelty. At their first meeting the Dean and lyners had to declare "that sundrie malicious and deboschit personnis of this toun" slandered and blasphemed "the guid establischit ordour of the Letter of Gildrie", particularly at their dinner tables "to the greit disgrace of the Deine of Gild and his counsell in presence of strangeris". It was decided that if any were found guilty of slandering the Dean and Council in future they must be punished and fined. Next day a Merchant, Robert Broune, agreed that if he should slander or blaspheme the new order of things he might be banished from Glasgow losing his freedom as a burgess of the city "and he nevir to injoy na benefit within the samin".

This would have been a harsh penalty. There is no indication that any erring guild brother was actually outcast from the city for criticising the Dean or the Letter of Guildry. It has been argued that the malicious and debauched persons who did criticise were reforming Presbyterians and that the Dean and the Merchants stood for Roman Catholic, or at least Episcopalian, reaction— that the Merchants, not all of whom were actual traders, were simply the conservative "Establishment" of the town, while the Craftsmen had represented Progress and Reform in the rivalry between the two ranks which led to the Letter of Guildry. This idea seems to be quite baseless. It is true that Archibald Heigait, the first clerk, belonged to one of the few Roman Catholic families that are known to have survived in Glasgow half a century after the Reformation, but two names in the first list of Merchants and their "assisters" were those of Protestant ministers.

Perhaps it was fortunate for the Guildry that it was founded at a time when the Protestant Archbishop of Glasgow had very little power. He soon regained the right to choose the town's Provost and bailies from short leets submitted to him, but the archbishops, though they were still lords of Glasgow, never seem to have had any similar control over the election of Deans of Guild and Deacon Conveners.

In that first list of Merchants and their assisters there are 214 names. A similar list for the Craftsmen has 373. Thus the two ranks were not very unequal in numbers. It is true that in the city's government the Merchants were a little more than equal in practice. Though, according to King James VI's ruling, there were to be as many Craftsmen as Merchants among the town Councillors, the Provost, two Bailies (out of three), the Dean of Guild, the Treasurer and the Master of Work who (like the Dean Convener) were additional town councillors *ex officio* were always Merchants, so that their rank had an assured majority. But, essentially, both ranks of the Guildry were privileged people, the organised middle class of the city. Presumably the craft lyners of the Dean of Guild's council joined with their Merchant colleagues in defending their dignity against "slanderers and blasphemers". In the troubled generations of religious controversy and civil war after 1605 Glasgow became a staunchly Presbyterian town, and there is no reason to think that its Merchants, as a whole, thought differently from other citizens about politics and church affairs.

The Merchants had their hospital in the Briggait (Bridgegate) the short street leading from the Saltmarket to the old Glasgow Bridge at the foot of Stockwell, and it was attracting endowments. A hospital in that age was not primarily a place for the sick. It was rather an almshouse for pensioners who had no other home. From the first, no doubt, the Merchants' Hospital provided such shelter, but most of the assistance was by way of pensions or pre-cepts (occasional grants) paid to "decayed" Merchants or widows and daughters in distress who were living elsewhere in the town. The first recorded endowment was a ground annual of forty shillings Scots given in 1602 by John Mure, Skipper for "the poore merchants that feirs God within the said citie to be stallet in the almous hous biggit in the Briggait", that is, for resident pen-sioners. It is interesting that this first bequest to the Merchants was made by one who two years later is one of the Commissioners for the Crafts. Other ground annuals, feu duties and sums of money were given or bequeathed from year to year.

The Letter of Guildry provided regular sources of income in the entry money of Merchant Guild brethren and in Dean of Guild court fines. There were also fees for the use of the Merchants' mortcloths—velvet palls for covering coffins on their way to the grave. In 17th and 18th century Scotland there had to be a pall of this sort at every well-conducted funeral and many kirk-sessions relied on the hire of mortcloths to provide money for poor relief. The Merchants had their communal palls.

They also drew "Bucket money"—8s. 4d. paid by each new burgess, which was shared between the Merchants and the Traders. This was intended to provide a primitive form of fire service. When at least the upper storeys of most houses were built of wood fires were frequent and dangerous. The Merchants and Trades Ranks had the duty of providing leather buckets which every householder could use when he was threatened with fire. From time to time the Town Council had to urge them to repair their old buckets and supply new ones, but the bucket money was usually treated as ordinary revenue till the Merchants' House gave up its share in 1807, when the first effective public fire service was set going.

The oldest surviving account book of the House is for 1624. It shows an income of £3,174:10:2d (Scots) and expenditure of £2,957:9:4. Part of the money was spent in pensions, though the oldest roll of pensioners, twenty-four years later, shows sums ranging only from 10s. to £5 (Scots) quarterly, amounting in all to £66:16:8—presumably £267:6:8 per annum.

The House was, in fact, able to invest money in its first half century in spite of the long wars of the Covenant, first against Charles I and finally against Cromwell, in which Glasgow lost both men and wealth. By far the largest legacy received by the Merchants at this time came from the formidable Zachary Boyd, minister of the Barony, who denounced Cromwell to his face in a sermon when the English conqueror visited Glasgow. The gift of £1,000 (Scots) offered the House its first direct link with education in Glasgow, for which it was later to do a great deal, for the money was to be invested to provide a bursary for a Divinity student at Glasgow University, if possible a Merchant's son of the name of Boyd.

With this and other sums land was bought in and around Glasgow. By far the most important of these possessions were the lands of Easter and Wester Craigs, acquired in 1650 from Sir Ludovick Stewart of Minto, the embarrassed head of a family which gave six provosts to Glasgow and to the coinage the lady who was the first model for Britannia. The Craigs, bought for 23,250 merks Scots (£1,291:13:4 sterling), stretched east from the glen of the Molendinar Burn into what is now Dennistoun. The House soon sold Easter Craigs but part of the western lands—the rocky ridge opposite the Cathedral—remained its oldest property, apart from the stone reliefs, till our day. They were to be developed first as a public park and then as the Glasgow Necropolis, but in the 17th century the House had farming tenants in Wester Craigs who bring into the records a whiff of Covenanting history.

In January 1680 "my Lord Dean of Guild and brethren of the Merchant Ranke" received a petition from David Monteith and John Cuming, tacksmen of the Craigs Park, asking for a remission of rent. The previous summer they had had crops lying in their barn and barnyard enough to pay what was due but then came the fight at Drumclog and rising of the Western Covenanters against Charles II. Armed men descended on Glasgow, first rebels and then the King's forces, "who, without any order or Licence came at thir pleasure, quartered in the park, did draw the stables, trampled, spoiled and brocked the corne, took up quhat was readie thrashin to thir horse in great quantaties and sent thir horse upon the growing grass and corne, and trampled and abused the same without controlment, most shamfullie, ther being seven score of the rebells horse on the grass and corne four nights besyd the King's troupe and uther troupes and companies of dragounes, and by the proviest [Provost's] order ther was at one time nyne bolls of corne given and a command to lett none of the King's troupe want corne, for quhilk we never got any satisfactione". It was duly agreed that a year's rent need not be paid.

In fact the House was now facing a crisis. It had been spending too much and receiving too little. The years of Cromwell's rule had scarcely been a prosperous time for Scotland, but in Glasgow they had been a great age of building. It was then that the fine baroque home of the University took shape in the High Street. Possibly this stimulated the Merchants' ambitions. Their hospital in the Briggait was said to be decaying. It was decided to "re-edify" it—tradition says—after designs by Sir William Bruce of Kinross, who, as architect to Charles II, was later to lay the foundation of the great age of Scottish classical building. More than seventy years later John McUre described the result with enthusiasm.

"It was rebuilt in a most stately manner in the year 1659, Sir John Bell, late provost, being then Dean of Guild. It is of length from east to west seventy-two foot, the steeple thereof is on height one hundred and sixty-four foot, the foundation is twenty foot square: it hath three battlements of curious architecture above one another and a curious clock of molten brass, the spire whereof is mounted with a ship of copper, finely gilded in place of weather-cock.

"The gild-hall, which comprehends the breadth and length of the house, is beautified with the gilded broads [boards], names descriptions and sums mortified for the use of the poor old members of the Merchant rank; likewise a large written broad with scripture direction how to buy and sell with a safe conscience. The hall is illuminated with fourteen chess [sash]* windows together with the apartment for the dwelling of four poor old men. The steeple hath a stately bell, being ten foot in circumference, which rings for the behoove of the churches [and] meeting of the Merchants House". Behind the hospital was a large flower garden.

The spire is still one of the finest things on the Glasgow sky-line as one looks north and east from the bridges. But it is all that remains of what must certainly have been an exceptionally attractive

---

*Sir William Bruce is said to have been the first to introduce this type of window in Scotland.

building—all, that is, except the two reliefs now in the modern
Merchants' House, and another stone, rediscovered only in 1945,
when a building in Parliamentary Road was being demolished.
This stood at the entrance to the old hall with an inscription—gilt
in its day, though now the gilding is gone—which declares in Greek
and Latin that the hospital was founded "by the pious liberality
and at the cost of the Merchants of the city of Glasgow in the year
of the common era 1601 [or possibly 1501, since the dating is
obscure]. It was rebuilt, enlarged and adorned by renewed generosity in 1659. Whoever gives bountifully to the poor lends to
Jehovah and he will return his gift to him." The stone is now in
the Old Glasgow Museum (People's Palace).

The new hospital was a fine thing, but within a year it was
proving to be unexpectedly costly. The Merchants found that it
had absorbed a good part of their investments. All the members
of the Merchants' House were asked to subscribe, with the promise
that those who did so would have a prior claim to pensions if they
fell into need. This was the origin of the House's Gold Books
which contained the names of the first subscribers and later became
the recognised record of membership.

But the yield of the first subscriptions was disappointing. The
times were uncertain. King Charles II had just returned to his
throne in London, and though his Restoration had been welcomed
with joy in Scotland whence it brought about the withdrawal of
Cromwell's English garrisons, the new Government quickly proved
to be expensive. The Dean of Guild had to turn to the Town
Council for help. He met with sympathy. It was recognised that
"now the steiple of the said Hospitall is to be raised, quhich will
prove far more profitabill to the toune than to the Hospital"—
presumably as an ornament of the city—it would be "a shame and
disgrace" if it could not be completed. The town, too, had little
money to spare but it gave what it could, on condition that the
Craftsmen should have similar help if they came to rebuild; and the
spire was duly finished.

Perhaps the Merchants' difficulties were partly due to the nature
of their investments. In those days, when there were no banks and
actual coined money was scarce, even the landed gentry were very
ready to borrow from all who had capital. The House had made
loans on bond to an impressive series of landowners, beginning
with the Countess of Glencairn, whose husband had led a rising in
favour of Charles II. As too often happened, the lairds were not

always able to pay their interest. The Town Council itself owed the House £2,000 Scots. By 1676 the revenue of the House had actually shrunk. Two years later, before the Covenanting troubles cut off the rent from Wester Craigs, pensions had to be reduced by one third "till it pleas God to increse the House stocke"—£500 more was being paid out than was received in income.

This was, indeed, the one period of Glasgow's known history before our own day of planned overspill, when the population of the city actually fell. There are other echoes in the House's records of the troubles which brought about the decline. In 1682 Provost Sir John Bell and Bailie Robert Corse assigned to the Dean of Guild and his Merchant Councillors all the fines which should come to them for "Disorderlie baptismes, marriadges, keeping of hous or field conventicles, withdrawing from the public ordinances" [or worship]—in fact from the persecution of Covenanting Presbyterians in Glasgow. Evidently the Provost and bailie were doing something to salve their consciences, though it does not appear that the House actually received any money as a result of this gesture. Next year it was laid down that the Dean of Guild, his council and electors must take the anti-covenanting Test, and in 1686 King James VII and 11, who was purging town councils of his opponents, nominated the Dean for the next year—the only case of such Government interference in the House's history.

The hard times did not end with King James's fall. In 1694 the House was supervising the raising of a tax of thirteen dollars per head on all "fenceable men"—those of an age to fight—to meet the cost of 44 recruits raised by Glasgow for King William's wars. Two years later it was decided to invest £1,000 sterling—a very large share of the House's capital—in the new Company Trading to Africa and the Indies on which Scotland built hopes of colonisation and commerce which were disastrously disappointed at Darien. The century ended with terrible years of famine when the crops failed throughout Scotland and other parts of northern Europe. At the height of this crisis, on the 9th May, 1699, it was unani-resolved by the House "that the haill poor belonging to the Toun be maintained". Five Merchants were chosen to act with a committee of five members each from the Town Council, the Trades House and the Kirk Session "to cast on a subsidie for the maintenance of the poor". Perhaps the losses of Darien may have had something to do with a decision that the families of lawyers should no longer draw help from the House "in regard the wryters in

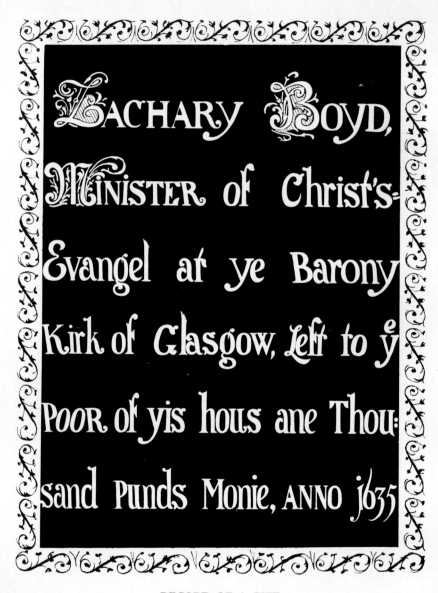

ZACHARY BOYD, MINISTER of Christ's-Evangel at ye Barony Kirk of Glasgow, Left to ye POOR of yis hous ane Thou-sand Punds Monie, ANNO 1635

RECORD OF A GIFT

This board in the Merchants Hall commemorates the Mortification by
Zachary Boyd, Minister of the Barony of Glasgow, of £1,000 Scots

Glasgow [the Faculty of Procurators] keep a box of their own and give the Merchants poor no pairt therof."

In these first difficult hundred years of the Merchants House, however, Glasgow had been laying the foundations of an expansive history. It had provided itself not only with handsome new buildings but also with its own harbour for sea-going ships at Port Glasgow. In 1705 merchants were solemnly warned by the House that they must not lay up or fit out their ships at any other port on the Clyde "except in case of necessitie". The House was already helping to operate a scheme for giving help to "poor and decayed seamen", financed by a levy of eight pence in the pound on sailors' wages.

In their dealings its members were guided (one hopes) by those "Scripture Rules to Be Observed in Buying and Selling" which were displayed on a "broad" in their new hall, as they still are in the present one.

"First take heed", the inscription runs, "that you do not discommend those commodities that are very good, which you are about to buy so that you may bring down the price of the commoditie and get it for less than it is worth * * * Prov. 20. 14. 'It is naught, it is naught, saith the buyer: but when he is gone his way, then he boasteth' * * * So should not the seller over praise or commend a commoditie when it is naught."

Buyers are not to protest that they will not go beyond a certain sum when, in fact, they are prepared to pay more. They are not to give counterfeit money "though you yourself took it for commodities", or to use false weights in selling. They should pay promptly. "It is the badge of a wicked man in Scripture not to pay his debts," in Psal. 37. 21. "The wicked borroweth and payeth not again."

The merchant must not monopolise any kind of goods "that by that means you may sell the commoditie at your own price: this is a meer oppression, destruction to a Commonwealth and to all trading". He must not take advantage of the other man's mistakes; "as suppose you should come to a shop and buy so many yards of cloth, or the like, and he should give thee more than is thy due, or take less money of thee than is his due, you shall take no advantage of him, but restore it again". There must be no buying or selling on the Lord's Day. It is wrong to take advantage of a poor man's need by giving a low price for what he has to sell. "Be not among the first that shall raise the price of a commoditie * * *

When you are found to be deceitful in your dealing do not justifie your deceit".

Finally, the merchant must not buy or sell "those things which are not fit to be bought or sold". He must not buy or sell stolen goods, or "monuments of Idolatrie * * * as Crosses, Beads and Images and Crucifixes", or trade in men for slaves. He must not sell spiritual things. He must not sell himself "as Ahab did to work wickedness". "You must not sell those things that are of no other use but to commit sin * * * as for to sell stuffe to paint harlots' faces is a sin, because it is for no other use but to commit sin in the using of it".

Some of this is stern advice, as stern as "the iron laws of economics" to which later generations of traders used to appeal, but the Scripture Rules probably had an influence on the proceedings of the Merchants' House long after the century which set them up in its hall.

CHAPTER IV

THE HOUSE IN THE MERCHANT CITY

THE eighteenth century is a leading age in Glasgow's history. It was then that, for the first time, it became a great place of business. Soon after the century began it was called by an admiring visitor "the beautifullest little city I have seen in Great Britain"; but it was, indeed, a little city with not much more than 12,000 people. Eighty years later the population was nearer 70,000 which made it not only the second city of Scotland but a great town by the European standards of the time. And Glasgow's wealth came in the main from trade, not from manufacture as it was to do later. Its great men were merchants—the Tobacco Lords, who made it, for a while, the chief centre of their trade in Europe, and the merchants of West Indian sugar.

It was natural that in a merchant city the Merchants' House should be specially important. Probably it was lucky for Glasgow that the official organisation of its merchants had kept an independent life of its own much more successfully than the older merchant guilds of other Scottish towns. Nearly all important burghs, to be sure, were managed largely by men of the Merchant rank, who provided the provosts (except where these were local lords or lairds) and at least half the town councillors. But in many of them —Aberdeen, Dundee and Edinburgh for instance—the councils had practically swallowed the old guildries. They appointed the deans of guild not (as in Glasgow) from a leet named by the Merchants but by their own choice. They had absorbed most of the guildries' property. In Edinburgh an entirely new Merchant Company was founded in 1681, to begin with as a drapers' guild, but it had very little part in the management of the city.

In Glasgow, however, the two bodies that made up the Guildry, the Merchants and the federated Crafts were just rising to the height of their influence after a century of official life. Their position in the town's affairs was emphasised by the Scots Parliament in 1705. The city was seriously in debt. To save its credit it was granted a new source of revenue, twopence Scots (a sixth of a penny sterling) on each pint of ale sold. For the town council this was a great boon and privilege, but it was laid down in the Act that the Merchants and Trades should join with Parliamentary commissioners in veri-

27

fying the debts to be paid with the money. Time and again when
the Town Council was in difficulties—over the need to raise money
for fortifications during the Jacobite rising of 1715, over the building of a new quay at the Broomielaw, over the cost of Prince
Charlie's requisition in the 'Forty-five—the Merchants House
was asked for its approval of what was being done.

The House soon learned to feel that it must be ready to state
its views on all important public questions affecting the city. In
1768 it could claim that "it is the right and privilege of this House
to be informed of every Bill proposed to be brought into Parliament
by the Magistrates and Council, by which the rights and interests of
the Inhabitants of this City may be affected, before application is
made to Parliament". The House did, in fact, have a say in most
important city matters not only through the Dean of Guild and other
magistrates and councillors who were Merchants but also with a
voice of its own.

In the early part of the century, however, it had its own share in
the crises of the time.

There were the anti-Union riots of November and December
1706, when, for weeks on end, Glasgow was more or less in the
hands of mobs protesting against the passing of the Act which was
to merge the Parliament and Kingdom of Scotland with those of
England. It is often said that the Union was approved in Glasgow
which was to benefit by free trade with England and the American
colonies; but in fact the change was violently unpopular, though the
attitude of the city's Establishment was rather uncertain. When the
first article (or clause) of the Act was passed in Edinburgh on
November 4th Glasgow's representative, Hugh Montgomerie of
Busby—of course a Merchant—opposed it. Three days later
Montgomerie's brother-in-law, the minister of the Tron Kirk,
preached a famous anti-Union sermon ending with the words,
"Up and be valiant for the city of your God". The streets filled
with protesting crowds. The deacons of the Trades saw the Provost,
John Aird, and demanded that the Town should petition Parliament
to abandon the Union project.

Provost Aird was a notable and respected figure in the Merchants House and the City. He had been three times Dean of
Guild and is said to have been responsible for the House's Scripture
Rules for buying and selling. His portrait, still prominently displayed in the Merchant's Hall, commemorates an important legacy
to the House. In 1706 he was probably one of the few convinced

supporters of the plan for the Union, but he evidently did not find it safe to say so publicly in this crisis. Instead he explained that it would be unwise to "address" the Parliament lest the famous grant of 2d. on the pint to pay the city's debts should be withdrawn. A few days later, when the anti-Unionists had armed themselves, smashed the Tolbooth windows and sought to see him again, he took refuge in a neighbour's house and hid in a collapsible bed.

"But the Hand that smote the men of Sodom with blindness when they would have rabbled the angels protected him from the many-headed monster", wrote Daniel Defoe, the novelist of "Robinson Crusoe" and an agent in Scotland of the English Government. Aird escaped and took refuge in Edinburgh, where there were troops to protect the Unionist authorities. It was John Bowman, Dean of Guild, and himself a future Provost, who took the lead in the hard task of trying to restore order. The burgesses, Merchants and Craftsmen, were, in effect, the only police force of the town. The Dean and Deacon Convener summoned them to mount a continuous guard. Every householder was to appear for this duty or send a substitute; even Merchants and Craftsmen, not actually on duty, were to join in quelling disturbances. But it is obvious that there was no enthusiasm for the work.

John Bowman and the Deacon Convener then set off to Edinburgh with an Anti-Union address, which was duly presented to the Parliament. Guard and petition together did not end the excitement, however. An armed party from Glasgow actually set off for Hamilton. They believed (wrongly) that an anti-Union army was gathering there—the Duke of Hamilton was the chief hope of the anti-Unionists. The riots subsided when troops, under the Duke of Argyll's brother, rode into Glasgow, but they revived again when the soldiers left and scarcely ended till the Act of Union was passed.

Nineteen years later, another Dean of Guild, John Stark, was arrested with the Lord Provost, Bailies and Deacon Convener when a mob sacked the house of the local M.P., Daniel Campbell of Shawfield, in protest against the new Malt Tax which Campbell had supported in Parliament. With the other magistrates, the Dean was soon released, though the city had to pay heavy damages to Campbell, its most successful merchant, with which he was able to buy the island of Islay from a fellow clansman. Danger came to Glasgow again with the 'Forty-five rising, when the Merchants House was convened to consider a petition to the Magistrates and

Town Council "setting forth that this city is threatened to be attacked by a [Jacobite] force which they are in no condition to resist, and that the inhabitants and their trades and dwellings are in imminent danger of being exposed to irreparable losses and inconveniences". The magistrates and council were asked to approve the choice of a body of trustees, including eight eminent Merchants "upon the approach of any such force to meet with their Leaders and make the best terms possibly they can, for saving the city and its trades and inhabitants from those dismal consequences."

In fact the trustees had to meet not with "a force" or its leaders but with a letter from Prince Charles demanding £15,000 and with his agent, John Hay, of Restalrig, sent to receive the money. They bargained pretty effectively with Mr. Hay, persuading him to take only £5,500, and the House agreed that "as necessity has no law", those burgesses who had money should make contributions on the understanding that it would be repaid by the people of Glasgow "according to their respective ability".

This was on September 27th, 1745. At Christmas, Glasgow saw the Prince himself and his little army on their retreat from Derby. He was received with no enthusiasm, for this was a thoroughly Presbyterian, Hanoverian city. He took another levy of goods from the town, the debt duly approved later by the Merchants House, and marched out in a week to win his last victory at Falkirk. Glasgow was not to see the front of active war again till the German bombers struck at it in 1940.

The Town Council was not alone in facing financial difficulties in these years. The Merchants House, too, had reason to be worried about its resources. A committee appointed in March, 1746, concluded "that the provision for the maintenance of the poor of the Merchant Rank is extremely scanty and small and that there is no ffund for supporting and defending the just rights and privileges of the fair traders", and that is, of the Merchant burgesses themselves. Resources for these purposes might be considerably increased, the committee thought, if "all traders in the place who are willing to contribute", were admitted to membership of the House. It would seem that, in spite of the terms of the Letter of Guildry, which evidently intended that all respectable Merchant burgesses should be members—indeed that they must be members as a condition of their right to trade freely—the Deans of Guild had acquired the right of nominating those to be admitted. The reigning Lord Dean, John Brown, offered to abandon this power, provided that the House ruled that his successors must do the same.

In these circumstances some changes in the House's Constitution became possible. It was decided that all traders "of a fair character", who were willing to pay five shillings sterling immediately and four shillings yearly, should be admitted "as the only members of the Merchants' House". In distress such members and their indigent widows and children were to have the first claim on the House's charity.

The Letter of Guildry had, in effect, given the Dean of Guild two councils—the Lyners, four Merchants and four Craftsmen, who with the Dean formed what has since been called the Dean of Guild Court and also that body of twenty-four Merchants chosen by the Dean himself who were to join in nominating candidates for the deanship and to be his advisers in the affairs of the Merchant Rank.

In future, it was now decided, all Members of the House should have a share in choosing this second council. On the second Wednesday after the election of the City Magistrates in October, the House was to meet. The Dean himself would then choose twelve councillors. The next stage of the election sounds strange to people of this century but was very characteristic of old Scots ideas about the election of committees. The Dean was to arrange the names of all the remaining Members in twenty-four leets, twelve consisting of overseas traders and twelve of home traders. The Members of the House would then vote to choose one man from each leet. These twenty-four, with the Deacon's own twelve, would form the Council of the House. And the Council, with the Dean, the Lord Provost and Merchant bailies, would choose (again through leets) the names of three candidates for the Deanship to be submitted to the Town Council for their final election.

These changes in the rules of the House, with some minor ones, had to be submitted to the Town Council for its approval. This was given on condition that all the House's Members must be burgesses and guild brethren before matriculating in the new form. Eight years later the House appointed the first of a long series of important standing committees. This committee on the Books and Affairs was to meet four times yearly and to consist of the Lord Dean, the Lord Provost and three other Members. It was, in fact, a form of executive.

The Merchants House was strengthened financially and its Members were given a greater chance to take part actively in its management. But its character was slightly changed. It could scarcely claim, even formally, to represent all burgesses who were traders. Merchants who were not prepared to pay the special contributions, remained outside it, though, in theory at least, "the Dean of Guild and his Council" could still compel them to come in. In 1771 the payment was consolidated into £4 sterling of entry money, and in 1792 it was raised to £10:0:0.

Through the years ahead, as Glasgow grew richer, the great men of the town took a leading part in the activities of the House. There was Lord Provost Andrew Cochran, who had guided the city through the troubles of the 'Forty-five and from whom Adam Smith, the greatest of Scotland's economists, learned much about the practical working of a trading community. There were the Tobacco Lords, who developed and controlled the city's most prosperous business, several of whom served on the Council of the House. There was Archibald Ingram, Lord Provost and twice Lord Dean, one of Glasgow's first industrialists, a pioneer of the business of textile printing which was to be immensely important to the West of Scotland in the age of cotton which followed that of tobacco.

The House took a specially active part in the improvement of navigation on the Clyde, still in the Eighteenth Century a broad, shallow stream, which no sea-going ships could use much above Dumbarton. In 1755 it promoted a Bill in Parliament for the building of the first Clyde Lighthouse, on the Little Cumbrae. Two years later it supported a Member, John McCaull, in pushing a plan for the deepening of the river, which forecast what was to be done nearly twenty years later. In 1767 it encouraged a scheme for the Forth and Clyde Canal, which was to give the city an outlet to the North Sea. It supported early plans for giving Glasgow a water supply other than the wells the old city had relied on, and for lighting the town. Even before there were steam driven factories it concerned itself seriously about the cost of coal supplies. It began to press for a regular post to London through Carlisle—something still unknown in 1781. Again and again, in years of scarcity, it concerned itself with the supply of meal for the poor and even pressed for free trade in corn, an almost revolutionary idea in that century when grain-growing landowners and farmers were carefully protected.

JAMES EWING
Lord Dean of Guild, 1816-17 and 1831-32 by J. Graham Gilbert, R.S.A.

The year 1767 is an important one in the House's domestic affairs, for it was then that it chose a Collector who was not an active Merchant to be its chief official, *under* the Lord Dean. To begin with the Collectors had been members of the Dean of Guild Court. Later they dealt with the House's finances and business, being rewarded by a percentage of the money they drew in. Now no Member of the House was prepared to take on this work, no doubt because it was becoming rather more arduous, and James Hill, "Writer in Glasgow", was appointed at a salary of £28 per annum. He was the founder of a respected Glasgow legal firm (now Hill and Hoggan) and was the first of a Merchant House dynasty. His son, his grandson and a great-grandson were to follow him. His grandson's great-grandson now holds the office. The Collectors have had a marked influence on the House's development over almost two centuries.

As the city prospered, the House began to receive more substantial legacies and gifts. The first, indeed, came as early as 1715, from James Govan, £627:1:8d. sterling, which was the Merchants' proportion of "one thousand ginnies in gold laid by and enclosed in a bag sealit with black wax with the seal of the Gally". Then there was property in the town left by Lord Provost John Aird which fetched £480 in 1752. A mortification by a prosperous Glasgow printer, Robert Sanders, of Auldhouse, gave the Merchant House Directors much work for generations to come. He left £611 sterling and his lands of Auldhouse (near Pollokshaws where his house still stands) to provide for the apprenticing of poor sons of Merchants or Craftsmen burgesses, and to found a divinity bursary at Glasgow University, both apprentices and students to be chosen by the House. This may be said to have been the beginning of a continuing interest in technical education. There were other substantial gifts for the aid of Merchants and their families in distress.

The help the House could give was still very modest by modern standards, though highly valued by those who received it in the conditions of the time.

In 1755 it was found that the funds had increased sufficiently to allow the grant of pensions of £100 Scots to three men and of £60 Scots to two others. All were to have been "men of credit" and business in the city, over fifty years of age, who had fallen into poverty. Three widows of Merchants were also to receive £100 Scots each. By 1786 the enrolled pensioners, supported from

c

general funds, were 15 men and 40 women, receiving in all £382:16:0 sterling, besides 23 men and women who received pensions from special mortifications and precepts, or grants for a particular emergency ordered by the House, or by the Dean of Guild personally.

But as the century reached its last quarter, Glasgow's first great age of mercantile prosperity was coming to an end. The tobacco trade—imports from the American colonies, exports to the Continent—depended on the Navigation Acts which laid it down that colonial goods must be carried only to British ports and in British ships. The war and revolution which converted the colonies into the United States of America put an end to all such restrictions. Henceforth American tobacco could be shipped direct to any part of the world. The position Glasgow Merchants had won as its chief importers and re-exporters in Britain quickly lost its meaning.

The House supported recruiting for the American War by agreeing that all men who joined the new Glasgow Regiment, which was being raised in 1778, should be made burgesses and guild brothers without payment when they were discharged, and that the families of any who died on service should have this privilege. But the day of tobacco was over. Soon the House had to consider the feeding of the poor in the distressed city. Glasgow Merchants had to look for another staple trade. It was for this purpose that the Chamber of Commerce, which has been a partner of the House in many activities and often (as now) has operated under the same roof, was founded in 1783. The new basis of the city's business was to be another American product, not only for trade but for manufacture. Cotton was now to be king.

CHAPTER V

THE AGE OF REFORM

IN spite of the hard times that Glasgow had passed through during the American War and after there was a certain optimism in the air before the 1780s ended. Business was reviving again. And there was a good deal of sympathy in Glasgow with the political ideas that lay behind the successful American Revolution. A Glasgow professor, John Millar, was the foremost teacher of liberal theories about parliamentary Government and constitutional law, on which the Americans had largely based their new republic. A former Glasgow Professor, Adam Smith, had published his great book, "The Wealth of Nations", which was to be a bible of capitalist free enterprise for more than a hundred years. Political reform and economic experiments were in fashion when the centenary of the "Glorious Revolution", which put reforming Whigs into power, came round in 1788. For half a century a wind of change was to blow through the world quite as persistently as it does in our day.

For a body like the Merchants' House in a city like Glasgow this state of things raised special problems. The House had been created largely to preserve the trading privileges of Merchant burgesses, which were out of tune with the new economic ideas of *laisser-faire*. In some ways its constitution was almost mediaeval. Yet Glasgow was a centre for new things, for the growing Industrial Revolution and expanding world trade as well as for new ideas. The leaders of the House were immersed in these developments.

The House had to keep one eye on the future and the other on the past, but its forward-looking eye was usually the more active of the two. From time to time it still tried to check trading by "unfreemen", which was contrary to its original rules and privileges but was constantly growing, yet, in the main, it welcomed change. Very characteristically it thanked William Pitt in 1788 for standing up for the rights of Parliament by insisting that the Lords and Commons had the power to decide on a regency during George III's illness "thereby asserting one of the most important rights of the People". This was Whig doctrine, but, conveniently enough, Pitt had been asserting it against the Opposition Whigs at Westminster.

Pitt himself had had ideas about parliamentary and political reform, and the House had discussed proposed changes in the sett (or constitution) of the self-perpetuating Glasgow Town Council, approving most of them, but on condition that "the undoubted rights of the Merchant rank should not be in any way impaired". It had also approved the first moves towards an important municipal change which was to create police commissioners elected by householders. It continued its attacks on the Corn Laws looking forward to "that happy period . . . when the landed as well as the commercial men of the Kingdom shall see their true interest in permitting the free importation and exportation of corn at all times" (1786). Meanwhile it demanded that special regulations which tended to raise the price of oatmeal in Scotland and especially in Glasgow above the price in England should be abolished—"any distinction in Laws to the prejudice of Scotland, more especially in such as relate to the Bread of the People is an intolerable grievance" (1791).

The political atmosphere was changing however. The French Revolution was welcomed at first because France seemed to many people in this island to be moving towards parliamentary government of the British kind. But soon there was alarm. The French deposed their King and defied Europe. What were thought to be French ideas—they were often, in fact, those of an Anglo-American, Tom Paine—began to seem dangerously popular to Pitt's Government. Groups of reformers organised themselves into Societies of Friends of the People which, ominously, had working class members.

In December, 1792, the House found it disturbing that its clerk, George Crawford, was "acting as Secretary to one of those Societies, which have given occasion to the present alarms with respect to the peace of the country". It was decided that "Mr. Crawford's services shall be dispensed with", though he continued to draw his salary for some months. The House solemnly resolved "That we consider it as our duty, and the duty of every loyal Subject and good Citizen, sensible of the blessings we and our Fathers have enjoyed under the present happy Constitution, to declare to the world our firm attachment to that most excellent Constitution and our determination to maintain and support it, more especially as we are convinced that if any abuses have crept into it the Constitution contains in itself the means of rectifying them".

The last clause suggests that at a time when Reformers, including a well-remembered Glasgow man, Thomas Muir of Huntershill, were prosecuted for sedition and exiled, some members of the House were still anxious to make it clear that, in their opinion, political change might not be a bad thing. But within two months Britain was at war with revolutionary France; it was a war that was to continue, with one short break, till Napoleon was finally defeated at Waterloo, twenty-seven years later.

With this, ideas of Reform became almost unmentionable for a while. The House gave its support to the Government and the war, though not without some discrimination. A motion in favour of peace negotiations was rejected in 1795, but at the same time the House advised the all-powerful "manager" of Scottish affairs, Henry Dundas, that if the Government wanted more men for the Navy it had better offer them better pay and a guarantee of discharge "within some reasonable time after the expiration of the term of their engagement or of the next arrival in Britain of the ship they belong to". In 1798, at a time of financial crisis, it joined with the Town Council, the Trades House and the Chamber of Commerce in urging that "a small Tax upon every kind of property or stock"—in fact a capital levy—would be the best measure that could be resorted to, "in order to make the burden fall equally upon all descriptions of People" at a time when "the very existence of this Country, and of all that is held valuable in Society, depends on the issue of the Contest" against "the boasted threats of an insolent foe".

In 1803 when a French invasion seemed possible, £500 was voted towards the cost of raising a volunteer corps in Glasgow—with the caveat "that nothing but the strong necessity and extreme importance of the measure could induce the House to appropriate any part of their funds to any other but charitable uses."

Four years earlier £500 had been pledged in support of Town Council plans to procure food for the people of Glasgow and in 1801 it was urged, not for the last time, that there should be no distilling of grain while supplies were short. The House was "impressed with a strong conviction of whisky's injurious tendency, not only as it respects the Manufactures of the Country and the morals of the People but also as it will materially abridge the comforts of the lower orders of the Community whose resignation and fortitude under the heavy pressure of a general scarcity have been eminently exemplary". A similar address to the Prince Regent in 1811 declared that "Your Petitioners are filled with fearful apprehension when they consider how much Grain and Potatoes have been lost and injured by the severity of the weather and also when they consider how unable the labouring classes of the Community will be to provide the abolute necessities of life at advanced rates, while the wages they are receiving are lower than last year's, when provisions were cheap and in plenty, and when, even at that time, a voluntary contribution to a considerable extent was found indispensably requisite to supply the wants of these classes, many of whom could not get employment owing to the stagnation of trade".

The long war was drawing to an end, however, and the movement towards reform of many kinds was soon to take life again. One man's influence on the House seems to have been particularly important in those years. He was James Ewing, twice Lord Dean of Guild (in 1816-17 and 1831-32), one of the most active and enterprising Members in its history and an outstanding benefactor at his death.

James Ewing (called 'of Strathleven' from the estate to which he finally retired) was a type of what many Nineteenth Century Glasgow business men most wished to be. The son of a prosperous West India Merchant, he went from the City's Grammar School to Glasgow University at the age of 12. He was already making a fortune for himself when he succeeded to his father's business. In his dealings he was said to be keen; he was certainly very successful and gave money generously for all sorts of good causes. Before he became Lord Dean of Guild at 41, he was already a town councillor actively interested in education, in the first Glasgow Savings Bank, in the fearful problem of the new industrial poor. This last interest made him a friend and disciple of the great minister of the Tron Kirk, Dr. Thomas Chalmers, who tried to prove practically that urban poverty could be dealt with by the Church.

It was James Ewing who persuaded the Glasgow Town Council to abandon the burgess oath which excluded some Dissenters from public life. In most things he was a moderate reformer, but, though intensely interested in politics, he never tied himself to a party.

An experience in 1820 must have left its mark on him. After the pitiful "Radical Rising" of that year the Government sent commissioners from London to apply the savage law of treason, always so unpopular in Scotland that no native court could be trusted to act on it. James Ewing found himself chancellor (*anglice* foreman) of the jury at the trial of James Wilson who had been tricked into carrying a broken sword towards Glasgow (which was said to be in the hands of a force of Reformers) but had turned back after walking eight miles. The jury found him guilty on one count of the charge but recommended him to mercy. The Government, however, wished "to make an example" and the bewildered man was duly hanged and quartered. The city and most of the jurymen were horrified; they had been convinced that Wilson would be reprieved. Though others concerned in the case were execrated it is said that Glasgow people had too much confidence in Ewing to blame him.

James Ewing's political career had a typical end. He was Glasgow first choice for the reformed Parliament of 1833, but at the next election he refused to pledge himself to vote against the Duke of Wellington's short-lived Tory Government—on the ground that no M.P. should ever give general pledges. He lost his seat and settled down again as a business man, a public-spirited citizen and finally a country laird. It was the sort of record that mercantile Glasgow most admired.

He first appears prominently in Merchant House affairs as the champion of a particular kind of free trade. The East India Company had a monopoly of British commerce beyond the Cape of Good Hope; goods from or for not only India but also Arabia, Persia, China and the Far East generally had to be carried in its ships or by its licence. Kirkman Finlay, the most powerful and enterprising of Glasgow merchants and cotton manufacturers had done more than anyone else to break through Napoleon's ban on British trade with the European continent. He was ambitious to put an end to the much older British rule which prevented merchants and shipowners from trading freely in Asia. In Glasgow, James Ewing was his chief supporter in this campaign. Together they no doubt inspired a petition by the Merchants' House to the House of Commons in March, 1812, when the East India Company's charter was about to be renewed, asking "that no Monopoly be granted of the Commerce and Navigation to the countries Eastward of the Cape of Good Hope, but that the Trade may be free and open, in the same manner as other branches of Commerce, not only to the Port of London, but to all the other Ports of Great Britain and Ireland".

Trade with India was duly thrown open, and the first Glasgow ship reached Calcutta in 1816; but fourteen years later the House

again petitioned for free access to China, where the East India
Company retained its monopoly till 1833.

James Ewing had no dread of peaceable change. He was deeply
attached to the Merchants' House as an institution and his first
conspicuous act as Lord Dean was to write a brief record of its
history. In contrast, his second, in 1817, was to support a proposal that the House's old Hall in the Briggate should be sold.
A committee was appointed to consider the question of " improving
the Property".

"That the Merchants' House of such a great commercial city
should have a place of meeting suited to respectability of this
Corporation there could be but one opinion", it reported. "The
present Building was renewed in its present form so far back as
1659, which is more than a century and a half, and when it is considered what was the state of the city at that period—how small
was the number of the population and how restricted the extent of
its Trade, compared with the present situation of the Town, it must
be admitted that such an Establishment conferred the highest credit
on the public spirit of the Merchants of that day . . . A very
material change, however, has taken place . . . The Bridgegate,
which was then the most respectable and fashionable part of the
Town, has now become the residence chiefly of the inferior classes,
with an awkward access and a still more objectional vicinity".

The sale of the Hall, the committee stated, would be profitable.
It would open for new building a useful (if not sociably very
desirable) strip of land between the Briggate and the Clyde; and
the expanding city needed all the new housing it could get.

"A site ought to be chosen which would not only be more
productive for the rent of the attached building but in all respects
be preferable for the occupation of so respectable a body. Such a
situation, your councillors are satisfied, may easily be procured
in a genteel and central part of the Town". . .

It was agreed that one part of the old building must be kept in
the House's possession—the steeple, which was "an ornament to
the City". Some thought that it should be stipulated that any
plans for new buildings must show off the steeple from its base;
"but as the lower half consists of a naked square tower, and as the
whole elegance is confined to the upper part above the clock, it was
considered a matter of no moment, or rather than it was advisable
to conceal the bottom".

THE N

with the Bridge of Sighs and Glasgow Cathedral in the

POLIS

From *View of the Merchants House of Glasgow*, 1866

The House accepted all these proposals with an assurance from the Dean of Guild that he had personally raised £2,000 by the recruiting of new members; this, with the price to be got for the old property, would provide funds for the building of a new Hall. It seems that the Dean of Guild Court was now pressing new burgesses to enrol in the House, as it was no doubt entitled to do under the Letter of Guildry, but had not, in fact, done for a long time past. At the next Annual Meeting, when James Ewing was succeeded as Lord Dean by a famous cotton manufacturer, Henry Monteith, the House formally thanked him "for his eminent services during the period of his holding office" and voted him "a piece of Plate, value Fifty Guineas, as an honorary mark of their appreciation and gratitude".

To those who have a feeling for old Glasgow the abandonment of the original Merchants' Hall will seem one of the less happy moments in the House's history. It was an early part of the process by which Nineteenth Century Glasgow destroyed the best relics of its own past. It set a precedent for the University's desertion of its fine old home in the High Street and the consequent conversion of gardens and fields which provided a "lung" for the centre of the crowding town into a mass of railway yards, and for "improvements" which banished all the old life and character of the High Street.

But in 1817 the Briggate, like the High Street, was degenerating into a shoddy slum though it was not yet overhung, as it now is, by great railway viaducts. The Hall had ceased to be a hospital for pensioners. Probably its garden could no longer bloom among the tenements. It is tempting to think that if it had to go it might have been replaced—as was, indeed, suggested at the time—by a new Hall facing the river and designed by one of the skilful Glasgow architects of the day, perhaps David Hamilton. This could have given distinction to an important piece of townscape between bridges.

More than a quarter of a century was to pass before the Merchants House found a new home of its own. Meanwhile it held its meetings in the City Council's hall. The famous steeple remained in its possession, rising from a not unseemly block of high housing, Guildry Court. It was later enclosed in the city's fish market.

Though homeless, the House was as vigorous as ever in its comments on public affairs. In March, 1819, it passed an outspoken series of resolutions against a proposal to levy a tax on coal at the pit mouth:

"That it is the abundance and moderate price of coal to which the city of Glasgow and surrounding district have been chiefly indebted for the establishment of so many branches of manufacture; and that even a very small tax upon an article of which the consumption is so great, both for the purposes of machinery and among the labourers employed, would be very sensibly felt at present, and might be gradually rendered more intolerable, were the principle once admitted of taxing so important a necessary of life.

"That to the labouring classes of this country a tax on Fuel would be quite as severely felt as one upon Provisions, which every wise Legislator would at once reject as equally oppressive and impolitic.

"That for these reasons this House will adopt every constitutional means of resistance". . . . .

Scotland was shocked in 1826 when the British Government threatened one of her favourite institutions, the £1 note. A financial crisis had emphasised the weaknesses of the banking system south of the Border, where the Bank of England, with its special privileges, was the only great company permitted by law. Other banks worked under severe restrictions and could not have more than six partners, but all could issue as many notes as they liked. In these conditions hard times produced waves of bank failures when the notes of weak firms were suddenly found to be worth nothing. The smallest Bank of England note was for £5. Scotland, on the other hand, had three chartered banks besides a number of other companies with quite considerable resources. Their £1 notes were the usual means of payment in the country and were safeguarded by a clearing house system of note exchange between the offices. But in England, local £1 notes had a bad name. It was proposed to abolish them throughout the United Kingdom. There was a national wave of protest, to which Sir Walter Scott contributed his *Letters of Malachi Malagrowther*. The Merchants' House, too, sprang to the Scottish Banks' defence.

Once again Kirkman Finlay and James Ewing joined in proposing a series of resolutions. "The commencement of prosperity in this country", they argued, "was nearly coeval with the Incorporation of the Bank of Scotland in 1695". They quoted Adam Smith to show the importance of the banks for the development of Glasgow's trade and emphasised the confidence of the people in "a solid and judicious system of Paper Currency convertible on demand into Gold ".

"The exclusion of Small Notes from the circle, and the obligation of Banks to provide Gold [in place of £1 notes] would materially diminish their ability to accommodate the Public, particularly in times of scarcity and pressure when the aid is most required. . . . Any attempt to alter the established usages of this land, to which we have been so long attached, and under which we have so long thriven is uncalled for by our circumstances, is opposed to our customs, and must be injurious to our interests".

The opposition was successful and the Scottish £1 note was saved; nearly 80 years were to pass before the rest of the United Kingdom would have a similar currency. The Merchants' House remained suspicious of Government interference with the Scottish banking system and protested against the Act of 1845 which restricted the right of Scots' banks to issue notes without a fixed backing in gold.

Meanwhile James Ewing had been taking a particular interest in what remained of the House's property of Wester Craigs. This consisted of the rocky height east of Glasgow Cathedral. Part of it was used as a quarry. The rest had been laid out as a sort of wild garden—the Fir Park, from which strollers could look down on the spreading city. A special committee was in charge of this little pleasure ground, probably the only thing of the kind in early Nineteenth Century Glasgow, except the historic Green by the river. In 1824 the Rev. Robert Stevenson McGill, Professor of Divinity at the University had been allowed to set up there the massive doric pillar carrying a colossal statue of John Knox, which still stands over the town. James Ewing helped to pay for this monument. Perhaps it was this which suggested to Mr. Ewing and the Collector of the House, Laurence Hill, a very active projector as well as a respected lawyer, the possibility of monuments of another kind. Four years later James Ewing suggested to the committee that the park should be converted into a burial ground.

It was, he thought, "admirably adapted for a Père la Chaise, which would harmonise beautifully with the adjacent scenery and constitute a solemn and appropriate appendage to the Venerable Structure in its front; and which, while it afforded a much-wanted accommodation to the higher classes, would at the same time convert a property at present unfrequented and unproductive into a general resort and a lucrative source of profit to a Charitable Institution."

Members of the House, it was stated, made little use of the park. At the same time the Barony parish "which now contains so many of the residences of our wealthier citizens" had no cemetery of its own "except the Crypt of the Cathedral". The rock was well suited "for constructing Vaults and Tombs of the securest description".

This was the origin of the Glasgow Necropolis, one of the most extraordinary architectural features of the city, and for generations a leading concern of the Merchants' House and its Directors. The plans for the lay-out of this dramatically placed burying ground were a matter of intense public discussion. They were completed by two eminent Glasgow architects, David Hamilton and John Baird, who recommended the building of the graceful Bridge of Sighs across the Molendinar Valley below the Cathedral. The leaders of Victorian Glasgow chose to lie in the new cemetery's forest of obelisks and temples. For many years the Merchants' House's charitable funds drew a considerable income from the unusual investment.

When the Necropolis was opened in 1833 its chief begetter, James Ewing, was both Lord Provost of the city and one of its M.P.s. The Age of Reform was in full movement, and, on the whole, the Merchants moved willingly with it. It is true that the House could oppose a Bill for extending Glasgow's boundaries on the ground that the value of its property might suffer (March, 1830) but it approved plans for Scottish legal reforms, as it was to do repeatedly in the future—on condition, however, that this would strengthen the work of the Courts in Glasgow, rather than in Edinburgh alone (April, 1830). But these were preliminaries to the great projects of parliamentary and municipal change which were now exciting the whole of Britain.

On December, 1830, a special meeting of the House was held to consider petitioning Parliament for a reform of the House of Commons which King William IV's new Whig Government was considering. Here, it may be supposed, James Ewing parted company with Kirkman Finlay, with whom he had acted so often. Finlay, long a Tory M.P., had been the great enemy of Glasgow Reformers and had no doubt inspired an address to King George IV ten years earlier when, at the time of the pathetic Radical Rising in the city (largely the work of *agents provacateurs*) the House had denounced "the daily attempts making by factious and designing men to seduce your Majesty's subjects from their allegiance, and by the degradation and abuse of one of our highest privileges— the liberty of the Press—to instil into their minds principles leading not only to discontent but even to insubordination and rebellion".

Now, however, the tone of the House's petition was almost radical.

"While the Population, Wealth, Enterprise and Intelligence of the Empire have for ages been steadily advancing, the real state of the Commons House of Parliament, which professes to represent and which ought to represent the People has been gradually and regularly retrograding from its original purpose, chiefly through the undue influence exercised on the part of the privileged classes by which they secure wealth and patronage to themselves and their followers, at the expense and to the great injury of the other and more numerous classes of society.

"The undue influence thus acquired by the privileged classes has now become so great as absolutely to threaten the overthrow of the Constitution; for while in many places those who have the ostensible right of voting are the slaves of some aristocratic family, in others their number is so inconsiderable that the Representative is, in fact, the mere nominee of one or two high-born or influential individuals. . . .

"These abuses . . . are peculiarly and strikingly manifest in the case of Scotland, where the return of Representatives in the different Counties is, with few exceptions, under the absolute control of one or two great families, and the election of Members for Burghs is exclusively confined to Juntos, who, in almost every instance, are self-elected".

When it was published the Reform Bill was welcomed by the Glasgow Merchants. But it was rejected in the House of Lords. The reaction of the majority of the Merchants' House was to petition King William to create enough peers to ensure the passing of the Bill (October 18th, 1831) though a minority felt "that a degraded House of Peers would become much worse than a useless burthen on the Country and would no longer occupy their place in the Constitution as the protectors of Liberty and Property against democratic fury on the one hand or against the acts of despotic power upon the other".

The King evidently agreed with this minority, for the moment, and the Whig Government fell. There was intense excitement throughout the island and in Glasgow great public demonstrations. At the fifth and last of the special meetings of the Merchants House during the crisis (May 11th, 1832) the House agreed to make two petitions, one to the King asking him to recall his Reforming ministers and the other to the House of Commons proposing that M.P.s should "withhold all supplies until the Bills pending in Parliament for amending the Representation of the People shall have passed both Houses, unimpaired and unmutilated, and shall have received the Royal Assent".

Such pronouncements from middle class bodies had, perhaps, as much influence on the King and the Tory peers as the demands of crowded meetings. Within three weeks the opposition to Reform collapsed. The old system by which, in Scotland, delegates from the self-perpetuating town councils in groups of burghs alone had a share in choosing an M.P., while in the counties voting was confined to lairds and their friends, came to an end. Householders where property was valued at £10 were now to be the voters and Glasgow was to have two M.P.s of its own, instead of sharing one with Renfrew, Rutherglen and Dumbarton. At the first election James Ewing was returned at the head of the poll.

In the years of James Ewing's second Deanship the House had been considering two other schemes of reform besides the Parliamentary one which had moved its members so deeply— reform of the Town Council and of the House itself.

It had wished to decide that in future Deans of Guild should be elected by all Members of the House, without any submission of nominations to the Town Council, that the system of leets for the choosing of Directors, with the Lord Dean's right to nominate 12 of the 36, should be abolished and that all should be chosen by the Members as a body. But, under the Letter of Guildry, changes of this sort could not be made without the approval of the Town Council, and the Town Clerk, James Reddie (who was no Reformer) had ruled that Parliament's consent would be needed before such a thing could be done.

A committee drawn from members of the Town Council, of the Merchants House and of the Trades House, had agreed on a modest scheme of reform for the Council itself. It was proposed that the number of councillors should be 40, each to hold office for five years. The Dean of Guild and Deacon Convener were always to be councillors. The Merchants House and Trades House were each to choose one other member each year, and each year the Parliamentary voters who were burgesses were to choose four councillors only. The Scottish Burgh Reform Act of 1833 swept aside a good deal of this canny planning, together with a later (and more surprising) proposal by the Merchants House that the Lord Provost should be chosen not by the Town Council but by the whole body of electors.

Under the new Act, the Dean of Guild and Deacon Convener held their place in the Council. The other councillors were to be elected by citizens (not necessarily burgesses) who had a parlia-mentary vote. Councillors need not belong either to the Merchants House or to the Trades House. The old rule that the Lord Provost and three bailies must be of the Merchant Rank disappeared, consequently "Merchant Magistrates" could no longer take part *ex officio* in the direction of the Merchant House as they had done.

The House was given the power to reform itself, and duly did so by instituting "an annual election of the Dean of Guild and all the Directors by the universal suffrage of every recorded Member . . . amounting to Twelve Hundred of the most respected Traders in Glasgow."

The Glasgow Guildry—Merchants' House and Trades House— had grown up, we have seen, both as part of the city's governing framework and as a group of friendly societies who looked after the interests of Merchants and Craftsmen and helped their own members in distress. The Houses had been tied to the Town Council in two ways; all the councillors were chosen from the two Ranks and the Council supervised their constitutions and made the final choice of the Lord Dean and Deacon Convener. Now, for the first time, the three bodies found themselves substantially inde-pendent of one another. From the first the Guildry, as a single body uniting both Merchants and Craftsmen had been rather a theoretical idea than a practical fact. Nothing was heard of it in 1833, or later.

The links between the two Houses and the Council were not completely broken. The Dean of Guild Court, containing both Merchant and Trade Lyners, continued to do essential work for the city by supervising new building, demolition and the laying out of streets. This work was specially important at a time when Glasgow was growing very fast; though it should be remembered that much of this development was in suburban districts (some of them independent burghs) over which the Glasgow Dean of Guild had no jurisdiction—a state of things which was certainly not for the good of the expanding city.

Free as it now was to manage almost all its own affairs, the Merchants' House had to work out its function as a body depending not so much on legal powers as on prestige and on its practical usefulness both to its own members and to the social health of the town. It was represented either by the Lord Dean or by one or more of its Directors on most of the public trusts and governing boards in which Glasgow was interested—for schools, hospitals, charities, roads, navigation. As before, it made pronouncements on public questions. It built up its own relief funds for its Members —and gradually for a wider public.

On the other hand one of the most important of its original purposes was gradually dropping out of sight. As Glasgow grew it had become more and more difficult to insist that all important trade must be in the hands of Merchant burgesses. The last serious attempt to punish all traders who were not freemen seems to have been made in 1755. Later in the Eighteenth Century (and still more in the Nineteenth) the atmosphere of the time grew steadily less sympathetic towards legal restrictions on traders.

The idea of discouraging "unfreemen" was not altogether forgotten. Under the Letter of Guildry this was the business of the Dean of Guild and his Court. Individual Deans could refrain from pursuing traders who were not burgesses, but an appeal to the Court from Merchants or Craftsmen who felt that they were suffering from what was strictly illegal competition could not be altogether neglected. The House, indeed, went so far as to inform the Commons in 1836 that it neither possessed nor sought "any monopoly of trade", but this could have been seen merely as a declaration that its Members, simply as Members, claimed no special privileges—which had been true ever since it had ceased to include all the Merchant burgesses of the time.

As early as 1821, however, it had refused to contribute to the expense of a law suit which the Dean of Guild of Cupar (Fife) was pursuing to try to obtain a ruling "that persons not entered as Brethren of the Merchant Guild have no right to open Shop within Burgh for the sale of Articles of Foreign Manufacture", and by the 1830s the attempt to insist on the payment of "fines" by Glasgow Merchant burgesses seems to have been abandoned altogether.

In the years after the Burgh Reform Act of 1833 had confirmed the Lord Dean's place on the Town Council and the authority of the Dean of Guild Court the House had to protest repeatedly (and successfully) against proposals which would have weakened the position of either Dean or Court. But the spirit of innovation waned for a time, and the House turned its attention to other matters—railways, for instance.

As early as 1808, long before any steam locomotive ran on steel, twenty guineas had been subscribed towards the survey for "a Rail Road" from the Monkland Canal to Berwick-on-Tweed, which must have been projected for horse-drawn traffic. The first call for a railway in the later sense came in 1836, when the House joined in a petition for "the level through line of Railway between Glasgow and Edinburgh" and against a proposal for a shorter line linking North Lanarkshire with the Union Canal which ran from Falkirk to the capital. It was, however, "most expressly declared that on no account whatever the House or its funds be made responsible for any expense whatever in consequence of so agreeing to petition".

By 1845 railways had fully established themselves. A great speculative boom in new companies was developing, and the House was usually careful not to commit itself as between rail projects. It did, however, express its "high satisfaction at the prospect which is now presented of the formation of a direct Railway communication between England and the City of Glasgow, by means of the Caledonian line" (by Lockerbie and Carlisle) and held to this in spite of a counter suggestion, no doubt by those who favoured a line through Ayrshire "that the more railways which have their termini at Glasgow the better for the community" (January 31).

On the other hand it took a sour view of a more purely local scheme, for the Glasgow Junction Railway, which, it was declared would "destroy the beauty and amenity of some of the most important streets in the City, endanger the lives of the citizens in its most crowded thoroughfares, particularly on the Glasgow Bridge, and by the constant flowing of sparks from the engines, greatly endanger the crowded shipping in the Harbour, and deteriorate in a material degree the Revenues of the Clyde Trust by interrupting the traffic on the River carrying to other and distant ports goods which would otherwise be shipped or transhipped at the Broomielaw".

D

These were evidently extravagant fears, though the old centre of Glasgow was, indeed, sadly gashed by railway building. The House had pressed for the creation of a Clyde Trust independent of the Town Council; when this was founded it provided three members. It took a strong interest in some projects of improvement that were not obviously economic, notable the "renovation" of Glasgow Cathedral, for which (most unusually where anything not directly charitable was concerned) it subscribed £500.

"The character of the City has suffered materially in the eyes of every visitor of intelligence and taste from the neglected and dilapidated state of the Cathedral, so different from the high state of repair in which the English Cathedrals are maintained, yet to none of which the Cathedral of Glasgow yields in point of antiquity or in Architectural or Historical interest. . . .

"The formation of the Necropolis by the Merchants' House and the judicious Regulations under which it has become one of the most interesting cemeteries in the Kingdom, if not in Europe, were based upon its vicinity to our great Civic Monument . . . All improvement then, upon the property in the neighbourhood concentrates the attention of the public upon the property of the Merchants' House; and no improvement . . . can do this so effectively as the completion of the Cathedral" (May, 1839).

As so often happened in Victorian attempts to "complete" mediaeval buildings, renovation involved some destruction which can be regretted now, but the Merchants' feeling for Glasgow's great church is as obviously sincere in the House's minutes as the argument in support is typical of their Victorian sense of the need to show that preservation could be profitable.

It was now necessary for the Merchants' House to find a home of its own again. For one reason and another it had not proved to be so easy to build a new hall on a "genteel and central" site as had been expected when the old Merchants' Hall was sold. The House seems to have met comfortably enough as the guest of the Town Council, and later in the City Chambers at the foot of the Saltmarket. But Glasgow Corporation (as it now began to call itself) felt the need of larger offices. It was decided to build these and also a new Sheriff Courthouse for Lanarkshire on a site between Hutcheson Street, Wilson Street, Brunswick Street and Ingram Street, in what is now very much the eastern end of the city's centre. The Merchants' House decided that its new hall should stand between the courthouse and the City Chambers. It was a handsome classical building designed by a firm of Glasgow architects, William Clark and George Bell, with an imposing hexastyle Corinthian portico facing Hutcheson Street and sculptured reliefs on the frieze.

Within it the House assembled the relics of its past which had been in store for more than a quarter of a century. The boards with the names of benefactors and the "Scripture Rules for Buying and Selling" were replaced or reproduced in a room which evidently sought to recall on a loftier, larger scale the House's old meeting place in the Briggate. The sculptured stones, with the reliefs showing Sixteenth Century Merchants and a ship were re-erected. Portraits and a new statue of Kirkman Finlay were displayed. In October, 1843, the opening of the new hall was celebrated by a public dinner.

When the House entered its new home it was just about to face the last change in its status which that Age of Reform would bring to it. Though the exclusive trading privileges of Merchant burgesses had, in fact, been slipping away through several generations they still existed in law. In October, 1845, the House was prepared to say again that traders ought to be Merchant burgesses, but by the end of that year the Glasgow Town Council had agreed to a change and the Dean of Guild Court had decided to suspend "the enforcement of the Law against persons who have commenced or carried on business in Glasgow from and after January, 1845", though it still claimed the right to penalise non-burgesses who had been trading before that date, on the ground that it would be unfair to refuse to protect the privilege of those who had previously "entered Burgesses" in due form.

Already, however, the Whig Government was preparing a Bill for the Abolition of the Exclusive Privilege of Trading in Burghs in Scotland. The House saw this with foreboding. In course of years, it declared, "a total abolition of the privileges hitherto enjoyed by Corporations", such as the Incorporated Trades and itself, "must result in the complete extinction of a Civic distinction of ancient standing intimately interwoven with the Public and Charitable Establishments of this City, and affording a qualification for the reception of Charitable Bequests vested in this House and other Public Bodies". As an alternative it was suggested that the entry fees paid by burgesses might be cut by half.

In spite of its anguished tone, however, this was rather a formal protest than a convincingly serious one. Its very wording shows that the House recognised that its chief function, though not its only one, was now the building up and administration of funds for the benefit of traders in distress and their dependants. In fact its greatest work in "the reception of charitable bequests" and their use had yet to begin when the Bill became an Act on May 14th, 1846.

What vanished then was the last shadow of the municipal Middle Ages.

CHAPTER VI

EARLY VICTORIAN

IN the hundred and twenty years since Merchant burgesses ceased to be privileged traders even in legal theory, the House has, indeed, found a new life. It has been able to aid its own members and the commercial community of Glasgow, to give help to other social groups, to provide education—all this on a scale that could scarcely have been contemplated in 1846. Then its "general stock" amounted to £36,555:11:9½d.; it had, in addition mortification-funds bequeathed for special purposes of just over £3,000. Its payments of pensions and precepts amounted to £1,174:6:8d. The comparable figures for 1966-67 are £393,826, £572,603, and £14,295; besides grants for education, to institutions and seamen and their dependants which amount in all to £31,486.

The Glasgow of 1846 was one of the most rapidly growing cities in an expanding world. Its population had much more than tripled itself since the century began—with its swelling suburbs it was now well over 300,000. The handsome new West End terraces which were the homes of many Merchants and future Deans of Guild reached out to the Kelvin. South of the Clyde new streets, some of them equally handsome, were breaking through the neat hedgerows of Govan Parish. New church spires were rising round the city; and also great new chimney stacks. The steam engine had drawn cotton factories into the town from the rivers and burn-sides where they had first sprung up to use water power.

Glasgow had its own growing works to produce the engines. On the edge of the southern suburbs a famous iron foundry, Dixon's Blazes, lit the night sky.

And with all this came smoke and spreading slums. The business centre of the city had not moved very far to the west when the Town Council, the Merchants House and the County Court-house Commissioners set up their new buildings between Hutcheson Street and Brunswick Street, but round Glasgow Cross and to the east population was pouring into the older buildings and into new shoddily built "back lands" behind these. At first this new prole-tariat had come mainly from the Lowlands, but the fearful potato famine in Ireland and the Highlands brought scores of thousands of starving refugees in the Hungry Forties to crowd into every possible living space from windowless cellars to garrets. The Merchants' House made special grants to provide food for the desperate poor, but in 1848 discontent, unemployment and political Charterism exploded into what looked like a revolutionary outbreak, when mobs raided gunsmiths' shops and the cry *"Vive la République"* echoed the Continental risings of that year. Business men, too, suffered "difficulties and distress", which the House attributed not only to the failure of the potato crop but also to the working of the Bank Acts that had restricted the operations of the Scottish banks.

By 1849, however, the clouds were beginning to lift. Glasgow was cheered by the first royal visit since the days of the Stewarts. The House addressed Queen Victoria with joyful loyalty:—

"In recognising in the august person of Your Majesty the lineal descendent of illustrious Princes who swayed the Scottish sceptre for a series of ages, we unite with all classes of our fellow-subjects in giving expression to those enthusiastic feelings of patriotism and attachment with which we bid you welcome".

To celebrate the occasion its pensioners were given a fifty per cent increase in their pensions for the current quarter.

In its expansion and its troubles early Victorian Glasgow had to adjust itself to life as a great industrial city. Nothing like modern Welfare Services existed. It needed hospitals and schools. It had its ancient University, already anxious to move from the slum-ridden High Street—indeed it claimed to have two, for the germ of what was to become first the Royal Technical College and now the University of Strathclyde called itself the Andersonian University. But all Glasgow's established public bodies had to look for means of growth. In an age of almost unrestricted free enterprise the State, and even the City Corporation, could do little for them. Commercial life was fiercely competitive. Fortunes could be made, sometimes quickly, but they could be lost as easily.

For such a society a body like the Merchants House was as important as it had been in the days when it had a more formal part in the direction of the town's affairs. It helped to canalise the impulse towards mutual help. This help could come only from private generosity and the active interest of men who had been able to gather money for themselves. In later days the image of the benevolent business man has often been caricatured. But it was, in fact, such men who made life in the Victorian city increasingly tolerable, who provided it with social organisations, from charitable societies for the unfortunate to colleges and churches.

Among Deans of Guild and Directors of the Merchants' House, who were successful business men, one finds a long succession who gave their time and money to social work. There were pioneers of help for the aged and for hospitals—notably William M'Ewen, the only man since James Ewing to have been re-elected as Dean of Guild for a second two year term—pioneers of slum clearance, like Sir James Watson, the first Glasgow stockbroker; pioneers of sanitation, like John Ure; reorganisers of municipal affairs, like Sir James King, William Walls and Sir James Bell.

The first business of the Merchants' House itself was, of course, to give a sense of security to its own members—to a social class, that is to say, which gets comparatively little attention even from the modern Welfare State. But by its influence and its members' work as well as by such grants as it was able to make it steadily supported the growth of the institutions and charities which Glasgow needed. The great flood of bequests and gifts which has multiplied its funds and expanded its work was only beginning in early Victorian times; but the very existence of the House drew gifts. Sometimes of an unusual kind.

There was, for instance, the case of Colin Campbell of Colgrain, who had owned a plantation in British Guiana in the days of negro slavery and had accepted a bill drawn on him there for £400. More than thirty years later, in 1862, he had never been called on to meet this debt and the holder of the bill could not be found. "Not wishing to retain money which does not really belong to him" he offered £672, representing the bill with accrued bank interest, to the Merchants' House on condition that he should be guaranteed against any further claims. The gift was welcome but the Directors, with proper caution, decided to let the money lie and gather interest until 14th July, 1865, after which no demand for payment could legally be made.

The greatest benefactions of that time, however, were those of James Ewing of Strathleven and James Buchanan. These were on a scale new to the House and opened up new lines of activity for its Directors. James Ewing bequeathed £31,000 to the House, £10,000 of which was to provide pensions or allowances for "decayed Glasgow Merchants", £10,000 for Merchants' widows and daughters in distress, and £10,000 to be spent chiefly "in educating, training and settling in business the sons of decayed Glasgow

Merchants". It was long before the estate was fully realised in 1906, but payments were made to the House over the years after his death, and the total finally received with accrued interest was £41,721:19/-.

The Directors recorded their sense of obligation in 1854.

"Under any circumstances liberality so great must have commanded their deepest gratitude; but they feel it to be enhanced by the recollection of the position which Mr. Ewing so long and honourably occupied as a Member of the House; a Merchant of Glasgow from his youth till his death, he never ceased to take the deepest interest in the Institutions of the City, especially in that which the Directors represent in which he was long an honoured office-bearer. By means of his liberality the Directors will be enabled to comfort the hearts and cheer the homes of many who, through the vicissitudes incident to commercial life, have themselves become the objects of that kindness which they or their friends in times of prosperity have shown to others, and, at the same time, provide for many the means of education on which their success in life so much depends."

Four years later another Glasgow Merchant, James Buchanan, left £10,000 (subject to his widow's life rent) "for educational purposes on behalf of the sons of decayed Members * * * and granting Bursaries to such of them as give evidence of future eminence". He also bequeathed £2,000 for the founding of a school for destitute boys towards which the House subscribed £500, appointing three of its members as directors of the Buchanan Institution.

Hitherto the House's chief educational interest had been in administrating the Auldhouse Mortification under which it paid apprenticeship fees for the sons of Glasgow burgesses. This had been the chief concern of one of its standing Committees. By the 1850s, however, it was finding that the employers of boys were no longer asking for such fees and that parents who applied for them were, by a legal fiction, able to spend the money themselves, perhaps not always for their sons' benefit. Their new experience of providing schooling for the sons of "decayed merchants" may have helped to turn the Directors' minds towards a possible change in the use of the Auldhouse funds which was to lead them into the support of a more modern form of technical education.

The Merchants did not enjoy their second home, in Hutcheson Street, for long. The Merchants' Hall there was evidently valued by others besides the House's members. Early Victorian Glasgow

THE EARLY VICTORIAN MERCHANTS HALL

in Hutcheson Street, occupied by the Merchants House 1843-70, now part of the Sheriff Courthouse. From *View of the Merchants House of Glasgow*, 1866

had too few public meeting places, and the handsome Hall was a favourite scene for balls and other entertainment as well as for more stolid and serious functions such as company meetings. A valued relic of the Eighteenth Century had been rediscovered and displayed there. In 1809 a grandson of Lord Provost Archibald Ingram, twice Dean of Guild (1757-58 and 1761-62) had offered the House a marble relief in which the kneeling Provost receives a wreath from the hand of the Genius of Glasgow, while three female figures, said to represent Commerce, Architecture and Civic Rule stand behind him. This handsome slab had disappeared and seems to have been quite forgotten when it was found by a Director in the cellar of the new Hall in 1859, and given a prominent place in the building.

But by 1867 the Court House Commissioners, who were the House's neighbours, were looking for more accommodation. Three years later an arbitrator decided that they should pay £176,673 for the Hall. Meanwhile the Chamber of Commerce, then at 6 Virginia Street, had agreed that the House should use its Hall while the Directors looked for a site for a new one. The House hung its portraits of former Deans and benefactors on the Chamber's walls. Its other relics were packed away.

Thus began a neighbourly association that has lasted to our own day when the Chamber is a long-established tenant in the Merchants House buildings. This third Glasgow "House" has always had close links with the senior body of Merchants. Many prominent Glasgow men have been Presidents of the Chamber either before or after their years as Lord Dean—there has been a general understanding that the two offices should not be held at the same time. On public questions affecting the business community House and Chamber have often spoken and acted together.

For the House continued to make petitions and pronouncements on public matters. It suggested improvements of navigation and port facilities on the Clyde. It asked for a decimal coinage (in 1855). It pressed for better postal services—but, on the other hand, in 1849 it "observed with much regret the contemplated change in the General Post Office, London, in reference to the transmission of Mails on Sunday * * * its immediate effect must be to increase the amount of Sunday labour in London as well as in many of the commercial Towns throughout the country, thus employing many individuals in secular duties that might be disposed to spend their time in connection with the Religious duties of that day".

In 1867, when Parliamentary reform was in the air the House petitioned (vainly) that Scotland should be given House of Commons seats in proportion to its population.

There was a special interest in legal reform. The House repeatedly urged the abolition of arrestment of wages on the ground that, relying on this, salesmen could tempt wage-earners disastrously into debt. In 1868 it was asking for the removal of the distinction between heritable and moveable property in intestate estates which was apt to put widows and daughters out of their family homes in favour of a dead husband's brother or cousin. It asked for arbitration in mercantile disputes as an alternative to litigation. In 1873 it protested vehemently against a proposal to introduce something like the English law of mortmain to Scotland —on the ground that this would tend to prevent "bequests of the wisest kind from flowing into the best of Charitable Channels."

By this time the House was involved in a legal dispute which seemed, for a time, to threaten the position of the Lord Dean in Glasgow Corporation and perhaps even its own existence as a historic body. In 1868 revised Regulations were adopted which stated plainly that "all persons who have paid Ten Guineas to the funds of the House and who have subscribed the Matriculation Book, and all persons who in time coming may be considered eligible by the Directors and who shall have paid the entry money of Ten Guineas or such other sums as may be fixed by a meeting of the Matriculated Members and who shall have subscribed the Matriculation Book, shall, *ipso facto* be deemed to be and to become Members of the Merchants' House of Glasgow." This was a formal abandonment of the old rule that the House should consist only of Merchant burgesses of the city. Burgess-ship had, in fact, lost its old meaning since neither voters nor Town Councillors themselves were required to possess it. The new Regulations were duly submitted to the Town Council in accordance with the Letter of Guildry, and were approved by it next year.

Meanwhile the House had been explaining and defending to a Scottish Law Courts Commission the value of the Dean of Guild Court. In the course of their dealings with the subject the Directors had come to the conclusion that the appointment of Clerk and Assessor to the Court needed to be reconsidered. The Clerk and Assessor was the Court's legal adviser. Under the Letter of Guildry "the Dean of Guild and his Council" were to elect a clerk annually. In fact from the first year of the Court's existence the man chosen had been one of the Town Clerks of the City Council. But there was now only one principal Town Clerk of Glasgow, and, in a city of more than 450,000 he was an exceedingly busy official. Moreover Glasgow Corporation owned a great deal of house property and was concerned in schemes of slum clearance and rebuilding which had to be considered by the Dean of Guild Court. It seemed wrong that the Court's chief official should advise it on plans for which his principal employers were largely responsible.

In 1872 the Town Clerk, Angus Turner, resigned. This seemed a good moment to make a change in the Dean of Guild Court. But here the history of two and a half centuries raised some very natural confusion in the minds of both Merchants House Directors and Town Councillors.

The Dean of Guild had come to have two councils each with a clerk of its own. The "council" of which the Letter of Guildry made most was the Dean of Guild Court itself, with its eight lyners, four from the Merchants' House and four from the Trades House. But the Lord Dean also had his Council of the Merchant Rank, long better known as the Merchants' House Directors; and this council too had its clerk. He was William Henry Hill who was also the House's Collector, the fourth of a family which had held the Collectorship from 1767 to 1837. Before his own appointment in 1866 W. H. Hill had compiled the House's history, *View of the Merchants' House of Glasgow.* He was an able lawyer and, no doubt, had a clearer view of the background of the problem which the House and the Dean of Guild Court were facing than any of the others who had to deal with it.

To begin with the Directors seem to have thought that the appointment of the Dean of Guild Court Clerk would be "put upon the same footing as that of all the officers elected by the Merchants' House,'. But that was a miscalculation. They were not the Lord Dean's "council" for this purpose. The City Corporation, on the other hand, assumed that the Court clerkship would belong of right to the Town Clerk they chose and that his fees for work in the Court could be merged in a Corporation Fee Fund.

At this point the very active Lord Dean, Patrick Playfair, publicly protested, no doubt with the advice and support of his Collector. He announced that he and his Court proposed to elect a clerk of their own choosing. For a time it seemed as if there might be a friendly compromise between the House and Court on one

side and the Corporation on the other. While both sides were
obtaining further legal advice the Corporation appointed an
interim Town Clerk, Andrew Cunningham, and the House and
Court decided that "to avoid unseemly conflict" the Lord Dean and
his Council should choose Mr. Cunningham as Dean of Guild Court
clerk till the end of the House's financial year in October. The
Lord Provost, Sir James Watson, was an active member of the
House and a future Dean of Guild. Evidentally he was ready to
see the Corporation's claim quietly forgotten.

But the man soon chosen as permanent Town Clerk of Glasgow
was by no means of this mind. He was J. D. Marwick, a strong
willed lawyer with firm ideas about the dignity of his office. He
came from Edinburgh, where the Guildry, more or less equivalent
to the Glasgow Merchants' House, had long ceased to be very
effectively active and had had to give up its claim to appoint members of the Dean of Guild Court, apart from the Dean himself.
Mr. Marwick—who, as Sir James, was himself to become a historian of Glasgow—evidently regarded the House as an anachron-
ism, which could become a nuisance. He insisted on his right to be
Clerk of the Dean of Guild Court. When the Court, with the
support of the House, elected a clerk of its own, James Roberton,
Professor of Conveyancing in Glasgow University, he refused to
hand over the official records and papers. The Court's work was
paralysed.

Again the useful Andrew Cunningham had to be brought back
to keep it going. Professor Roberton resigned. Mr. Cunningham
carried on his work for the Court, in the eyes of the House as
temporary Clerk and Assessor duly elected by the Court, and in
those of the Corporation as the Town Clerk's deputy—while the
two sides prepared to bring the whole problem before the Court of
Session. On this matter J. D. Marwick dragged his feet for two years.
Under his guidance the Corporation disputed the proper form of
procedure. Meanwhile two explosive charges were placed under the
feet of the Dean of Guild.

Though its own lyners had supported the Lord Dean throughout
the dispute, the Trades House was induced to state that the Town
Clerk was the best possible Assessor for the Guild Court and to
hint that the Merchants' House was exceeding its powers by inter-
vening on this question. Dean of Guild Playfair made a firm but
diplomatically friendly reply to this message which seemed to
isolate him and the House from their natural allies.

The second explosive may have seemed still more dangerous. Ignoring the Corporation's approval in 1869 of the Merchant House's new Regulations, Mr. Marwick argued that, having ceased to consist only of burgesses, the House was no longer legally constituted. A Dean elected by it was not qualified to sit in the Guild Court or in the Corporation itself. Conceivably indeed, even the House's right to its older funds and resources might be challenged.

This was a dangerous argument, however illogical it may seem, for there were Town Councillors who disliked the presence in the Corporation, *ex officio*, of the Lord Dean and the Deacon-Convener of the Trades. Perhaps it was lucky that the Dean who followed Patrick Playfair was a man capable of notably persuasive leadership, James King of Campsie. Speaking and acting in the Corporation on many matters Dean of Guild King made such an impression that he was later asked by the Councillors to allow himself to be elected unopposed as an ordinary member in order that he might be chosen Lord Provost. As the City's chief magistrate he was immensely successful, organising Glasgow's first great international exhibition in 1888. This was the best possible proof of the practical value to Glasgow of its *ex officio* Councillor. Yet, on the basis of Mr. Marwick's argument about burgess-ship every Dean of Guild who took his seat in the Corporation till 1885— including Patrick Playfair, James King himself and ex-Lord Provost Sir James Watson—had to meet a formal objection to his presence, though this was never pressed to the point of excluding him.

Meanwhile the case of the Dean of Guild Court Clerkship finally reached the Court of Session in 1876, when the Judge Ordinary decided that the Court had always had the right to choose its own Clerk and Assessor. This was total victory for the House and Court in a sometimes rather anxious comedy that brought to life a good deal of Glasgow's civic past.

The comedy was not quite over, however. Gracefully, Dean of Guild King proposed that Town Clerk Marwick should now allow himself to be elected Clerk of the Court. Mr. Marwick replied that he really had no time for the work and could accept the invitation only if the indispensable Mr. Cunningham could continue to act as his deputy.

After a decent interval Mr. Marwick withdrew altogether. At last the Court was able to choose a clerk completely independent of the Corporation, the Glasgow University Professor of Scots Law. Its organisation was strengthened. With the support of the

Merchants House it was safeguarded against the effects of an Act of Parliament which might have made it subject to Corporation control. The House had obtained for the Court everything that it wanted in 1869.

While the controversy was still seething the Directors were concerned with something more intimately important to the Merchants' House itself, the building of a new Hall. In 1873 they found a site that suited them, on the west side of George Square. This was becoming, unmistakably, the very centre of the city when the House sold one of its few remaining properties in land, at the Square's south-east corner, for the erection of a post office large enough to give the improved facilities for which the Directors had often asked.

The Bank of Scotland was preparing to build at the west end of the Square. It was agreed that the bank's new office and the Merchants' building, though ultimately the work of different architects, should conform to a general pattern. The architect chosen by the House was James Burnet, one of the most notable in mid-Victorian Glasgow. In four years a handsome block looked across the Square to the future site of the City Chambers, the Merchants House occupying the northern corner with West George Street.

Within this building John Burnet provided a lofty hall with an open pitch-pine roof. It was planned to display the House's portraits and the "broads" commemorating benefactors and their legacies. With its range of high windows it may have been consciously reminiscent of the old Hall in the Briggate. The building also contained committee rooms and offices both for the House itself and for the Chamber of Commerce, with other accommodation to be let to business firms: its cost—such was the value of money in the 1870s—was only a little over £32,000. The ancient reliefs which were the House's most historic possessions were set up at the entrance to the hall itself and the Ingram panel above the Directors' Room fireplace.

By October 1877 some of the offices were already in use, and on 21st November 1877 the Hall was officially opened at a dinner of Members, who had most of the city's leading personalities as their guests. Here was a visible sign that, thirty years after its old legal privileges had disappeared, the Merchants' House held its place firmly in the life of the City.

CHAPTER VII

FROM CRISIS TO WAR

LESS than a year after the opening of the fourth* Merchants' Hall, when the Directors of the House met there on October 1st, 1878 to make their decision on the nomination of a new Dean of Guild, Glasgow was on the edge of the worst financial crisis in its history. The House itself was in an unusual situation. The retiring Lord Dean, Sir James Watson, had to announce that John Muir, who had accepted nomination for the Deanship had withdrawn at the last moment on grounds of ill-health. Another candidate, James Stevenson, manufacturing chemist, noted for his interest in the civilising of newly discovered African countries and in working class housing, had been found. He was duly elected a week later.

But on October 2nd the newspapers announced that the City of Glasgow Bank had closed its doors. This was the youngest of the large Scottish banking companies and (apparently) one of the most enterprising. It had, of course, no connection with the Glasgow municipality. Its 133 branches were spread throughout Scotland and the Isle of Man, but most of its 1,270 shareholders were in Glasgow or the West of Scotland.

There had, of course, been Scottish bank failures before this one, though they were few compared with those in Eighteenth and Nineteenth century England, the United States and other countries. During the financial crisis of 1857 another big Glasgow company, the Western Bank of Scotland, had collapsed and the City Bank itself had closed down temporarily. But what distinguished the disaster of 1878 was the size of the losses, amounting to £6,000,000,* and the discovery that the failure was the result of fraud by directors who were to be imprisoned for falsifying accounts and using the bank's funds for their own purposes.

The shock was not merely a psychological one, destroying business confidence. Like all such Scottish institutions of the time except the three oldest, which operated under royal charter or Act

---

³Or third, if the building of 1659 is reckoned merely as a reconstruction in the Briggate.

⁴For an idea of what this sum meant in 1878 one may note that it was roughly twice the current valued rental of all buildings and land in Glasgow.

of Parliament, the City of Glasgow Bank was an unlimited company. Each of its shareholders was individually responsible for its
debts to the full extent of his own possessions. To Victorian business
men the very idea of limited liability had been deeply suspect.
The Merchants House had repeatedly protested against proposals
in Parliament which tended to make it available for banks and other
companies. But now, as the full extent of the City of Glasgow
Bank's losses became known uncertainty, depression and bank-
ruptcies spread throughout the West of Scotland. When the
resources of the weaker shareholders were exhausted successive
calls on those who still had some means of payment spread ruin
to new circles. Many members of the Merchants House were
reduced to poverty.

Perhaps it is not surprising that, less than a month after his
election, the new Lord Dean should have found himself forced to
resign because of a breakdown in health which may have owed
something to natural anxiety.

Precedent suggested that in a case of this kind the most junior
ex-Dean available should be brought back to the chair. This had
happened in 1868, when Dean of Guild John Ramsay had resigned
on being elected an M.P. But then the interim Lord Dean who
succeeded him had only four peaceful summer months to serve.
James Stevenson's successor would have the best part of a stormy
year. Sir James Watson may not have been sorry to discover that
a paragraph of the Letter of Guildry declaring that no Dean should
bear office for more than two years together seemed to exclude
him since he had retired only a few weeks earlier. In such a crisis
the business of a leading Glasgow stockbroker must have needed
all his attention. The previous Lord Dean, James King, was president of the Chamber of Commerce, and so unable to act. It was
left to Patrick Playfair, who had borne the brunt of the struggle
over the Dean of Guild Court clerkship to undertake what must
have been an anxious duty.

The situation was met with courageous vigour. The House's
resources from legacies had been increasing. It had just learned of
the splendid bequest of a Member, Samuel King, which was to add
more than £18,000 to its general funds.

It was decided that in spite of financial depression, more money
could be spent. All existing pensions and new applications for help
by Members were individually examined by the Directors. Some
pensioners decided that they could do without the House's help.

WILLIAM McEWEN
Lord Dean of Guild, 1869-70 and 1884-85 by Norman McBeth, R.S.A.

Most payments were actually increased. Accommodation was given in the new Merchants House building for the organisers of a city Bank Relief Fund. An ex-Dean, William M'Ewen, was perhaps the chief promotor of this charitable effort which distributed £400,000 among those who suffered most from the failure. Most of the House's Directors served on its committees. But years passed before Glasgow recovered completely from commercial loss and unemployment. It is significant that in successive annual reports till 1886 the Directors had to point out that some offices in the Merchants' Hall were still unlet. The Directors had been considering a proposal to double the entry fee for new members from ten to twenty guineas, but this was quickly dropped. It was finally adopted only in 1924.

It was not surprising that there were few large new gifts to the House during the 1880s. The great wave of large benefactions did not begin till the following decade and after, but many of them came from men and women who must have remembered the days when need was greatest. It is perhaps reasonable to suppose that, in the end, the experience of 1878 helped to strengthen the House for its work in the Twentieth century.

Meanwhile, however, the House was concerned to make the most of its existing charitable funds. Here again, William M'Ewen was a leading force. An Endowed Institutions (Scotland) Act had been passed in 1878, and this enabled the House to reorganise its old mortifications, the use of which was restricted by the terms laid down by benefactors. The yield of some of the gifts and bequests was very small. They were now augmented from the House's free resources so as to yield pensions of not less than £5 per annum. In 1883 William M'Ewen was re-elected Dean of Guild for a second two year term, largely to make it easier for him to carry his work further—though perhaps also in the hope that this universally respected figure would be able to put an end to the annual protest against the Lord Dean's presence in the Town Council; as in fact he did.

Under his guidance the House was able to raise the level of most of its pensions from £10 to £50. "In awarding pensions", it was stated five years later, "the Directors have to exercise much discrimination, and in this delicate and responsible duty they endeavour to give recognition to Members whose circumstances with age and infirmity call for aid, and their widows and young children, to whom the Directors deem the revenues of the House

E

for benevolent purposes are exclusively destined." There was another augmentation of many pensions in 1902.

By that time the House was able to take a wider view of its own good works. The city had fully revived and was expanding. The House demanded in 1886 that Glasgow should be allowed to grow officially by absorbing its suburbs. Perhaps a psychological turning point was the Jubilee of Queen Victoria, whom the House "as administrators of funds which commercial prosperity through many generations has generously bestowed for aid of the distressed, the widowed and the fatherless", addressed in June, 1887, acknowledging with satisfaction "the judicious and progressive principles which have characterised and the benign influence and efforts which have ensued from the legislation of your auspicious reign."

"Science and Arts", the address continued, "have made vast and unparalled strides; and discoveries, as wonderful as useful, have ensued, the result of which has been to augment the wealth of the nation and to carry comfort to the homes of the people. Religion and learning have been fostered. An acquaintance with and appreciation of the wants of the poor, largely promoted by the kindly interest of Your Majesty and Your lamented Consort, H.R.H. Prince Albert, have also during Your Majesty's reign been notably displayed alike by legislation ameliorating the conditions of the labouring classes and in improving the education of the people.

"No less notably has Your Majesty's reign been distinguished by wise and well conceived measures for removing restrictions and impositions which in former times fettered the free development of trade and navigation, of industry and manufactures. And while", the address concluded with cautious enthusiasm, "at the present time the outlook for the country is neither so prosperous nor the social conditions in all parts of the United Kingdom so satisfactory as your loyal subjects would fervently desire we nevertheless hope and pray that by the operation of economic laws the commercial depression which presently prevails may pass away and, by judicious legislation wisely administered, all reasonable grounds of complaint may be removed".

By next year this surviving spirit of uncertainty was almost gone. Glasgow had put itself on show with a great International Exhibition and with the opening of its Corporation's new headquarters, the City Chambers, rising into towers and domes without and, within, glowing richly with exotic marble and panelling.

Ex-Dean James King was its triumphant Lord Provost. It was as Sir James King, Bart, that the House brought him back as interim Lord Dean in 1894, breaking for his sake its old rule that the junior ex-Dean should take over when a Dean died in office.

And it was now that the House received a bequest which allowed it to give regular help to others besides Members, their wives and daughters. This was the Morgan Mortification amounting to over £60,000 left by John Morgan, of Springfield House, Bishopbriggs, "for the charitable objects and purposes of the House". The Lord Advocate advised that its interest could be put to "any good and pious use", in the terms of the Letter of Guildry.

It was soon to be followed by others which extended the scope of the House's charity. The largest and the most dramatically announced was the Inverclyde Bequest. The second Lord Inverclyde, head of the well-known Burns family of shipowners and himself chairman of the Cunard Company, was Lord Dean of Guild (1902-4) and died soon after leaving office. In December 1905 the Collector, W. H. Hill, reported to the House's Finance Committee a quite unexpected message from the late Dean's lawyers. Lord Inverclyde had made a formal Will which had already been published, but "while recently investigating the contents of a headboy which he had left in his business room at his office in Jamaica Street, Lady Inverclyde, his late Lordship's widow, discovered among a number of other papers a document apparently of a testamentary character written by his late Lordship and subsequent in date. * * * Her Ladyship, with whom were the present Lord Inverclyde and Mr. Timothy Warren, the family solicitor, at once handed over the document to the latter: but it appears that there is considerable doubt both as to its legal validity and effect, and in all probability these will require to be determined judicially. The writing * * * is in these terms:—

'I leave everything to my wife which I possess in Trust for her and the Trustees to be chosen by her.

'After her death I leave everything to the Merchants' House of Glasgow for the creation of a Fund to be known as the Inverclyde Bequest. The Income of this Fund is to be allocated annually by the Directors of the Merchants' House to charities or Institutions connected with Seamen or for the benefit of aged or infirm Seamen or their families. The term "Seamen" is to include all those who form the crews of merchants vessels."

'I wish the income of the Bequest allocated in the following proportions:—

'Seamen and Seamen's charities in Scotland—Two fifths.
           do.   Liverpool and
                               Manchester—One fifth.
           do.   Belfast—One fifth.
           do.   New York and
                               Boston—One fifth.

'I wish in particular that assistance should be given to deserving seamen who are in distressed circumstances who have been in the service of the Cunard Company or Messrs. G. & J. Burns * * *.'
(Signed) 'Inverclyde'."

This unusual will was duly formalised and confirmed by a special Act of Parliament in 1906, and on Lady Inverclyde's death the House received in 1926 "the largest contribution ever made to its funds" amounting, with an additional £1,000 bequeathed by the fourth Lord Inverclyde (Lord Dean, 1949-51) to £184,147. The income is distributed chiefly through associations or institutions for seamen, and sub-committees in Liverpool, Belfast and New York advise the House's Directors on its use in the specified ports outside Scotland. This may be said to revive an old tradition of the House, which showed a special interest in the troubles of seamen and their families as long ago as 1694.

The designation of Deans at this time suggest a changing social pattern. Among them have always been found both "self-made" men who had built up their own businesses and members of long-established Merchant families, but in the Eighteenth and Nineteenth centuries many were both business men and lairds, known by the names of their estates as well as of their forbears. In the 1860s John Ramsay of Kildalton was followed by Archibald Orr Ewing of Ballikinrain. Mr. Orr Ewing became a baronet in his later years. Among subsequent Deans several have been titled, including three peers. On the other hand Robert King of Levernholm (1904-6) brother of Sir James King of Campsie, was probably the last to take his style from his lands. He was also the only candidate proposed by the Directors in modern times whose election has been contested at an Annual General Meeting—apparently on the ground that the House needed new blood in its management of its affairs. It is very characteristic of the House's spirit of moderation and compromise that when he came to retire Mr. King should have proposed the name of his defeated rival, Thomas Mason, who himself became Sir Thomas after his years in the chair were over.

In 1905 Glasgow and the House gave a Prime Minister to the United Kingdom for the first time. Sir Henry Campbell Bannerman was a Member and the son of a Director and benefactor, Lord Provost Sir James Campbell. His Liberal Government which was to lay the foundations of the Welfare State and of centralised town planning caused the House some alarm, however. Some of its proposals were, indeed, unfortunate. Among them was the Land Values Taxation (Scotland) Bill of 1906, the final effect of which was to hold up house building in Scotland. The system was, in the end, to prove unworkable. Under the Bill Burghs were to be given the right to levy a tax on site values as well as the ordinary rate on rentals. Against this the House petitioned Parliament with logical vehemence.

"The object of the said Bill", it declared, "is to revolutionise the system of land assessment in Scotland by imposing a discriminatory tax against owners of landed property and of feu duties and ground annuals". The House, like other such owners, would be called on "to furnish information about a state of matters which does not exist, viz: the value for which this ground would sell if it had no erections upon it * * *

"The promotion of the present Bill is due partly to hostility to the private ownership of land and partly to the extent to which the Local Authorities who have taken up the measure have been increasing their expenditure and running into debt. In order to avoid the necesssity of retrenchment they desire to obtain additional revenue from a class which is limited in voting powers * * * "

In previous years the House had repeatedly and successfully protested against proposals which seemed likely to undermine the independence of Glasgow Dean of Guild Court. In 1909 came another, the Housing, Town Planning, etc., Bill which seemed likely to sweep away the Court's powers altogether in areas approved for redevelopment. Again the House petitioned Parliament, this time in conjunction with the City Corporation and the Trades House. With the help of local M.P.s an amendment was secured safeguarding the Court's jurisdiction.

It was in 1909 that the House obtained a special Act of Parliament for its own purposes, the Buchanan and Ewing Bequests Act, which gave a new form to part of its educational work. The Provisional Order of 1880 which allowed it to reorganise its minor

mortifications had also given it power to change the use of the
Auldhouse funds bequeathed to pay apprenticeship fees for the
sons of burgesses. Such fees, as has been seen, were no longer
needed. Henceforth the money was used to give suitable boys
education with a technical bent, chiefly by paying their fees for
Allan Glen's Institution.

Under the Buchanan and Ewing Bequests also the House was
paying school fees for the sons of "decayed" merchants or burgesses. But in this second case application for help from parents
and guardians had been falling. In the early Twentieth Century
it had become much easier to obtain free secondary schooling.
The new Act allowed the House to use the two funds to give grants
to Glasgow University and other colleges of higher education,
notably what is now the University of Strathclyde; to help students,
sons of Glasgow merchants, in research, and to encourage their
studies and training elsewhere.

Meanwhile the Merchants' Hall building was being extended
to provide office accommodation which would bring in additional
rents. The architect was John James Burnet, the more famous
son of the Hall's first designer. He added two storeys to the building, modifying the proportions of the Hall itself and perhaps
weakening the handsome balance of the West side of George
Square. The work was completed in 1909.

The House was jealously concerned for the relics of its past,
however. The Briggate Steeple, all that remains of the seventeenth
century Merchants' Hall, was repaired, and when in 1913, the
Town Clerk suggested its removal "with a view to the extension of
the Fish Market" the Annual General Meeting indignantly said
"No". The badge which had been used for many generations was
legitimated by a patent of arms from the Lord Lyon in 1912. One
of the old oak doors of the Briggate Hall and an oak chest made
from the beam to which the bell in the steeple had been suspended
were placed in the House's Committee Room.

The chest was a bequest from William Henry Hill, the Collector
and Clerk who had been the chief official of the House for 46
years. Mr. Hill's had been a constant influence which guided the
House towards the Twentieth Century without losing touch with
a past that reached back more than 300 years.

The Directors recorded "their high appreciation of his judge-
ment, his administrative ability and his uniform tact and urbanity.
To his constant concern to conserve the interests of the House and

uphold its traditions is due in no small degree to the regard with which the House is held by the community". His partner in the ancestral law firm, James Alexander McCallum, was appointed to succeed him.

With this date in October 1912 a chapter in the history of the Merchants' House may reasonably end. Fifteen months earlier, in a coronation address to King George V the House had prayed "that Christianity may advance and peace prevail among the nations: that Trade and Commerce may flourish and learning, Arts and Sciences increase and develop to the well being of mankind, adding lustre to the annals of your time". In 1914 Europe was at war. It was a new chapter not only for Glasgow but for humanity

CHAPTER VIII

THE AGE OF BEQUESTS

OURS has been a time as full of disturbance and change as any since the Seventeenth Century, when the organisation of the Merchants House was establishing itself in Glasgow. The Welfare State has come to birth, and we are apt to suppose that benevolent work of an older kind has lost its importance or has even ceased to be possible in its earlier form. Yet in the past half century the resources and many of the activities of the House have, in fact, expanded faster than they had ever done before. Its old task of providing for members and their families in distress has been as necessary as ever, but it has been able to give help also to people who would have had no claim on it in other days. Even in years of depression its financial strength has continued to grow. It has reorganised its machinery and its funds. The old Merchant Guild remains a necessary institution in the life of the city.

The war of 1914-18 did not, to begin with, affect the life and work of the House very deeply, though for a time its grants to public relief funds for Belgian refugees, men in the Forces and their dependents threatened to reduce what could be given in normal pensions. With other Scottish institutions the House had to protest against Government regulations under which the holders of the new War Loans or their heirs and the heirs of Scottish military officers (who were sadly many) had to apply to the Bank of England or English Courts in London for legal title to their property. It was only when a member and former Director of the House, the future Prime Minister, Andrew Bonar Law, became Chancellor of the Exchequer, that the necessary concessions began to be made.

But the flow of bequests to the House continued. Two were particularly important because they allowed it, for the first time, to give help to women who were not the widows or daughters of members. They were the legacies of three ladies, Miss Marjory Shanks Schaw, who died in 1915 and two sisters, Miss Mary Hamilton and Miss Hamilton L. Hamilton, whose mortification came to the House in 1916. Miss Schaw's bequest which, with a subsequent gift from her trustees, amounted to £20,000, made it possible to give pensions to Glasgow ladies over 50 years old, "who had seen better days", and Hamilton's Mortification of

THE MERCHANTS HOUSE BUILDING TODAY

£40,000 could be spent on help not only for women and children but also for "necessitous and deserving" men who, if they had been members of the House "would have been deemed worthy of its benefits". This set a pattern of expanding benevolence which the Directors encouraged other intending legatees to follow in years to come.

In 1917, the Lord Dean, Hugh Reid,* looked ahead towards the coming years of peace. He began a campaign to attract new members who would strengthen the House. He pressed the City to build homes for working people, and he foresaw that Members of the House and their families would have peculiar difficulties to face. Some, who had served in the Forces, would have to re-establish themselves in business or, if they were young men, would have to make a new beginning of their working lives. The Lord Dean proposed that a Merchants House War Relief Fund should be created to meet these needs. To found it he gave £10,000 in memory of his son, killed during the war.

As the plan was worked out the fund was divided into two parts, one to provide interest-free loans or grants for the establishing or development of businesses and the other to give pensions or other help. The first was to be terminable when the special post-war needs were met. The capital of the second was to be maintained and eventually merged with the general funds of the House.

This was a far-sighted and imaginative plan to strengthen a new generation in the business life of Glasgow. In practice, however, it had to meet peculiar problems during the 1920s, and 1930s, when business depression in the West of Scotland was almost continuous and not even the most enterprising and active could be sure of finding a foothold in trade.

In 1917 the Directors had received and approved a letter from a member, John Gray Buchanan, Chairman of the Metal Merchants Section of the London Chamber of Commerce, which looked at the developing state of trade with some foreboding.

"Government officials", Mr. Gray Buchanan wrote, "regard Merchants as an unnecessary adjunct to trade and propose to introduce the Cartel System—i.e. central agency for everything, eliminating the Merchant and the small manufacturer and substituting big combines".

5Son of James Reid, Dean of Guild when he died in 1894, who had begun life as a blacksmith's assistant and became head of the great Hyde Park Locomotive Works. Hugh Reid was made a Baronet in 1920.

The encouragement of the House's War Relief Fund no doubt helped young men (and also older ones) to make a new start, while it eased the lives of others who could not hope to reach again the sort of position in life they had held in 1914. But in the years of depression it was sometimes difficult to find suitable candidates for loans and grants which could lead to independence, even among Glasgow men who had no family connections with the House. By 1938 the terminable section of the Fund was almost exhausted, though it was not finally closed down till 1961. The permanent section is now used to raise the level of pensions granted by the House, the money value of which is now between two and four times as high as it was in 1918.

The House can seldom have been more useful than it was between the wars, when economic crisis struck at the lives of many in the business community and when there was a need for the renewal and expansion of a whole series of Glasgow institutions. Repeatedly grants were made towards the building or endowment of colleges, schools and hospitals. Directors had constantly to consider, with practical humanity and at the same time with detailed discrimination, applications for help from a widening range of men and women in distress.

New funds flowed in which could be used more freely than some of the older bequests. In 1921 William J. Chrystal left £10,000 "for such purposes as the Dean of Guild and Finance Committee may determine". Miss Rebecca Edgar's Bequest of 1925 was to assist "deserving widows in reduced circumstances, of men who, while not in business on their own account in Glasgow, should appear to the Directors to have been useful in carrying on the business life of the City". In 1933, Sir Frederick C. Gardiner (Dean of Guild, 1923-25), and his brother, William Guthrie Gardiner, created the Gardiner Fund, "in order that the Directors may be enabled . . . . to deal with more cases of those who have no membership claim in the House, direct or indirect, but who while not in business on their own account, have occupied important and responsible positions". The brothers and their trustees eventually added £8,500 to their gift of £10,000 On the eve of the second Great War of our time, a Director, Laurence Glen, left one-third of his estate—finally amounting to over £65,000—"for the general charitable and benevolent purposes of the House without any restriction for membership qualification". Other important benefactions of this time included £5,000, "to be used as the Directors think proper"—left by Dr. Robert T. Moore, Dean of Guild, 1925-27.

The second war was much more clearly anticipated than the first. In April, 1939, a sub-committee of Directors was already considering the safeguarding of the Merchants' Hall building against air raids—a quarter of a century earlier the idea of insurance against aerial attack had not been considered before August, 1915. The Directors approved plans for protection and fire-watching which involved much negotiation with the House's tenants and their employees. Inevitably the Briggate Steeple, the House's historic possession, was soon brought into the picture of war. In the 1920s and 1930s, a watchful eye had been kept on this relic of the old Hall, which for some purposes was in the care of the City Corporation; in 1921 a rather regretful consent was given when the Corporation decided that the steeple bell should no longer be rung daily, as it had been for nearly three centuries. Now the steeple, rising above the Fish Market, was an obvious stance for fire-watchers, but the Directors insisted that it should not be exposed to unnecessary damage. They were not much reassured by a reply from the secretary of the local Fire Prevention Committee, stating that he was sure none of the fire fighters would be inclined to advertise to the enemy the position of the steeple, "as their own framework would be of more consequence than a lifeless building". The Corporation was told yet again that it must take full care and responsibility.

Luckily none of the House's property suffered during five and a half years of war, and its portraits and other treasures which had been carefully stored, were duly returned to their proper places in 1945.

As the war years proceeded it was found that they gave an opportunity for some useful re-organisation of both regulations and work. Among the Directors was a man with the instincts of a reformer, John Dallas, who felt that the qualifications for membership of the House should be made clearer; that the arrangement for choosing Directors and the Committees which carried on the active work of the House, should be reconsidered, and that the system of paying pensions and the attention given to each case should be overhauled in a way which would ensure greater care for individual needs.

It was well that his campaign should have begun at a time when thoughts were beginning to turn towards the creation of the post-war Welfare State; in this way the House was able to fit itself to meet new situations. In the matter of membership the House had, in fact, been broadening its base—moving away, almost imperceptibly, from the insistence that all members should be independent business or professional men towards the acceptance of executives who might not always be proprietors, partners or directors of their firms. The Directors of the House were free to choose any who, "may be considered eligible".

In 1942, when Mr. Dallas's proposals were discussed, the Dean of Guild was, probably for the first time, a man whose work had been done solely as an executive on one side of an important firm; Sir Robert Bruce, former Editor of *The Glasgow Herald*.

It was decided that men "of known substantiability and good repute established in Glasgow, or in the West of Scotland with Glasgow connections", might become members if they were:

(*a*) in business on their own account "to a substantial extent, or in good practice in a recognised profession other than the Ministry", or

(*b*) Directors, managing directors, managers or other principal officers "in a considerable business, corporate body, or authority", or

(*c*) Men "of like standing and qualifications" established elsewhere in Great Britain who were sons of members, or were generally, "of recognised eminence or otherwise possessed of qualifications which in the opinion of the Directors would make them desirable Members of the House".

This was a wider foundation for the Twentieth Century and one which still preserves the special character and traditions of the Glasgow Merchants. In the nomination of members for election by the House as Directors new arrangments were made in these years to encourage the regular choice of a proportion of new men, without losing the advantages of experience in the work. Every member is free to propose names for election at the Annual Meeting, but to ensure that all vacancies are filled, the Directors are careful to nominate the required number of candidates. After some years of discussion and experiment the House formally recognised a tradition by which former Lord Deans remained Directors *ex officio*.

In 1942 the Directors were still grouped, as they had been for about a century, in three standing committees. Of these the Committee on Finance, Pensions and Adjustment of Business, which included all the ex-Deans, had long been almost the executive of the House for most matters. The other two, on Bursaries—in effect covering all the educational interests of the House—and on the Necropolis, were smaller and met less often. In 1943 a new Committee on Pensions was set up to deal with what was unmistakably one of the main functions of the House. Four years later this committee took over educational work also. The permanent Bursaries and Necropolis Committees passed out of existence, the bursaries being dealt with by the Pensions Committee and the Necropolis by the Finance Committee. All Directors were then able to specialise either in the management of finance and general questions or in the House's social work.

Indeed the Necropolis Committee had been losing its reason for existence. The idea of a "a Père la Chaise" made little appeal to Twentieth Century Glaswegians who had ceased to think much about cemeteries and the House could no longer draw any profit from what had once been its boldest investment. The Necropolis with its elaborate tombs was, indeed, a conspicuous feature of the city, but its owners were not sorry when in 1966 Glasgow Corporation took it over, agreeing to maintain it on condition that £50,000 was paid over by the House for its upkeep.

The new structure of committees was the first part of the reorganisation which was carried on into the later 1940s. The second part, also urged by John Dallas, was concerned with the administration of pensions. He was anxious that the fullest use should be made of the funds of the House which, during the War and just before it, when needs had been rather less pressing, had sometimes been allowed to accumulate. He urged that scales of payments should be adapted both to the rise of prices and to the development of State Old Age Pensions. Pensioners, he argued, ought to be visited in their homes by Directors who could know them and their circumstances. In 1949, shortly before the death of Mr. Dallas, the first Lady Visitor was appointed to maintain such contacts.

In a bequest to the House of £10,000 to establish the Simon Dallas Fund for Maiden Ladies, daughters of business men, "whose financial circumstances have substantially deteriorated," Mr. Dallas described the type of social situation he was most anxious to alleviate. "The reduced value of money, the heavy burdens of taxation and the limited income derived from small investments have changed the position of many maiden ladies of good education, and, without limiting the power of the Directors, I may say that the object of this bequest is partly to assist those, the amount of whose income may disqualify them for Government Old Age Pensions. The ownership of any capital, other than a dwelling house, in excess of £1,500 should be taken into consideration in deciding upon grants, and it is my wish that the pensioner be visited at least every second year by a Director of the House, and that grants . . . . be sent to the recipients each half-year by post and that such recipients be not required to call for payment".

Other important legacies came to the House at this time, including one of £19,400 from Dr. D. Johnstone Smith, and one of £38,800 from P. D. Ridge-Beedle. Both of these benefactors had been Members of the House (Mr. Johnstone Smith a Director) and each left the House free to use the money for those in need without membership restriction. On the other hand a grant of £10,000 from the Trust Funds of Sir George Arthur Mitchell, Dean of Guild from 1933 to 1935, was to supply grants to charitable institutions or associations in the City. The anonymous gift of £1,000 by an ex-Director in 1958 made it possible for all pensioners to be granted the means for taking a holiday.

A legacy of 1965 gave the House the William Clements Simpson Bequest Fund of some £20,000, which allows it to help "necessitous Christian widows or widows and unmarried daughters" of Glasgow merchants or professional men and to make grants to charitable institutions and organisations "operating in or near the city". In 1966 the House received from Mr. Daniel Duncan, a former Dean of Guild, and still a very active Director, investments to the value of £9,497, the income to be used for charitable purposes other than educational.

One of the most interesting legacies intimated to the House between the wars was that of George Craig, consulting chemist and chemical engineer, who left his estate, after payment of legacies, "for the upbringing, training and educating of orphans of Scotch parentage with the object of dissociating them from their surroundings (which could throw them back a generation) and making them worthy citizens, or eminent citizens if further help can effect it". This was an effort to deal with human problems of an exceptional kind. It has given the Directors a new sort of educational task—that of finding schools or opportunities of further learning for young people who find themselves facing difficulties which would deny them social opportunities which their parents might have been expected to give them.

It was not until 1959 that the assets, valued at £58,377, were received by the House. By this time it was found that the terms of the Will could not be literally carried out and it was necessary to obtain the authority of the Court of Session to a Cy-près Scheme to give effect to the obvious general intention of the testator. It was also necessary to consider how far the funds must be invested in trustee securities.

This led, in 1960-61, to a further reorganisation of the whole funds of the House. A Financial Adviser, Mr. John Dunlop, C.B.E., C.A., F.F.A., was appointed. After the Directors had obtained a favourable opinion from Mr. W. I. R. Fraser, Q.C. (now Lord Fraser, a Senator of the College of Justice), the funds were re-arranged in three groups—a "General Pool" of those which were not restricted to trustee securities and where there was power to spend capital; the "Hamilton Pool", where also investment powers were unrestricted, but capital must not be spent; and a Trustee Pool, including the great majority of special mortifications and bequests, where trustee securities must be held. The arrangements for this last pool were modified to take advantage of the wider power of investment of trust funds allowed by the Trustee Investments Act, 1961.

There was some temporary drop in the value of the House's funds as a result of these changes, but its financial affairs are more firmly founded than ever.

In these last years the House has, as usual, had other interests and problems. In 1935, 1944, 1949 and 1956, there were attempts, or the threat of attempts, to exclude the Lord Dean and the Deacon Convener of the Trades from the City Corporation. Since elected councillors have come to be firmly organised in parties, the position of *ex officio* members has sometimes been delicate. Deans of Guild have done their best not to allow themselves to be aligned politically. The existence of two genuinely independent voices representing an important side of the City's life can, in fact, be more valuable than ever.

In 1964, however, a Scottish M.P., Mr. William Hamilton, proposed to exclude *ex offico* members from the Corporations of the Scottish cities—Glasgow, Edinburgh, Aberdeen, Dundee and Perth. There were prolonged negotiations and it was finally agreed that Deans of Guild and their colleagues should retain their places on the city councils but with the right to vote only in committees, not in full council meetings. The change became law in August, 1965.

On the other hand the House did not protest when the creation of a new Clyde Port Authority broke its old links with the administration of Glasgow's river. The Clyde Navigation Trust, on which it had two representatives, and the Clyde Lighthouses Trust, on which it had one, disappeared under the new organisation.

With the creation of the National Health Service the endowed hospitals, which the House had helped to found or support, lost their independence and representatives on their governing bodies could no longer be appointed in the old way.

In 1948, however, the new authority for these matters, the Western Regional Hospital Board, invited the House to recommend individuals to serve on the boards of management of the various groups of hospitals. An active interest dating from 1787 when the House subscribed for the building of Glasgow's first general hospital, the Royal Infirmary, is thus continued.

In 1947 Mr. T. L. Grahame Reid, W.S. a descendant of the Hill family, who, for so long, provided the House with its chief officials, was appointed Joint Collector and Clerk with Dr. James A. McCallum. The following April Dr. McCallum died. He had helped to guide the House through a time of rapid social change. "His high sense of duty, courtesy and dry humour", the Directors' annual report recorded, "won for him the esteem and affection of all who knew him and, not least, those who were the beneficiaries of the House, to whom he was a wise, kindly and sympathetic friend". Mr. Grahame Reid became the sole Collector and Clerk. He is only the third to hold this position in the last hundred years.

The Merchants' House has had its succession of Lord Deans, each with his own claim to distinction in the commercial life of Glasgow. Three and a half centuries after its constitution in 1605 its beneficent work and its funds are still increasing and it is still able to speak, when this is necessary, for the commercial community it has represented so long.

THREE COLLECTORS IN A HUNDRED YEARS

Top left—W. H. Hill, LL.D., 1867-1912
Above—James A. McCallum, LL.D., 1912-1948
Bottom left—T. L. Grahame Reid, W.S., 1948-

DEANS OF GUILD OF GLASGOW

From the Date of the Letter of Guildry, in 1605

1	Matthew Turnbull	1605	1606
2	Archibald Faulds	1607	
3	William Sommer	1608	
4	George Master	1609	
5	James Bell	1610	1611
6	William Weems	1612	
7	James Bell	1613	1614
8	John Lawson	1615	1616
9	John Rowan	1617	
10	Colin Campbell	1618	1619
11	John Rowat	1620	1621
12	Colin Campbell	1622	
13	Matthew Turnbull	1623	1624
14	Patrick Bell	1625	
15	Matthew Turnbull	1626	
16	Colin Campbell	1627	1628
17	Patrick Bell	1629	1630
18	John Barns	1631	1632
19	Henry Glen	1633	1634
20	John Barns	1635	1636
21	James Hamilton	1637	1638
22	Walter Stirling	1639	1640
23	James Bell	1641	
24	John Barns	1642	1643
25	Henry Glen	1644	1645
26	Andrew Cunningham	1646	
27	James Hamilton	1647	
28	William Dunlop	1648	1649
29	John Graham	1650	
30	William Dunlop	1651	1652
31	James Hamilton	1653	1655
32	John Bell	1656	1657
33	James Campbell	1658	1659
34	James Barns	1660	
35	Frederick Hamilton	1661	1662
36	John Barns	1663	1664
37	Frederick Hamilton	1665	
38	James Pollock	1666	
39	John Walkinshaw	1667	1668
40	John Anderson	1669	
41	Frederick Hamilton	1670	
42	Robert Rae	1671	

43	John Walkinshaw	..	..	..	..	1672	1673
44	John Caldwell	..	..	..	..	1674	
45	Frederick Hamilton	..	..	..	..	1675	1677
46	Ninian Anderson	..	..	..	..	1678	
47	Robert Campbell	..	..	..	..	1679	1681
48	Hugh Nisbett	..	..	..	..	1682	1683
49	John Fleming	..	..	..	..	1684	
50	Robert Cross	..	..	..	..	1685	
51	George Johnston	..	..	..	..	1686	
52	Robert Campbell	..	..	..	..	1687	1688
53	William Napier	..	..	..	..	1689	1690
54	James Peadie	..	..	..	..	1691	
55	John Leckie	..	..	..	..	1692	1693
56	John Cross	..	..	..	..	1694	1695
57	John Aird	..	..	..	..	1696	1697
58	Robert Rodger	..	..	..	..	1698	1699
59	John Aird	..	..	..	..	1700	1701
60	Robert Zuill	..	..	..	..	1702	1703
61	John Aird	..	..	..	..	1704	1705
62	John Bowman	..	..	..	..	1706	1707
63	Thomas Peters	..	..	..	..	1708	1709
64	Thomas Smith	..	..	..	..	1710	1711
65	Robert Zuill	..	..	..	..	1712	1713
66	Thomas Smith	..	..	..	..	1714	1715
67	Adam Montgomery	..	..	..	..	1716	1717
68	Thomas Thomson	..	..	..	..	1718	1719
69	James Peadie	..	..	..	..	1720	1721
70	Gilbert Buchanan	..	..	..	..	1722	1723
71	John Stark	..	..	..	..	1724	1725
72	James Peadie	..	..	..	..	1726	1727
73	Hugh Rodger	..	..	..	..	1728	
74	Andrew Buchanan	..	..	..	..	1729	1730
75	William Cunningham	..	..	..	..	1731	1732
76	Andrew Ramsay	..	..	..	..	1733	1734
77	Arthur Tran	..	..	..	..	1735	1736
78	John Gartshore	..	..	..	..	1737	1738
79	James Robertson	..	..	..	..	1739	1740
80	George Bogle	..	..	..	..	1741	1742
81	Matthew Bogle	..	..	..	..	1743	1744
82	George Bogle	..	..	..	..	1745	1746
83	John Brown	..	..	..	..	1747	1748
84	George Bogle	..	..	..	..	1749	1750
85	George Murdoch	..	..	..	..	1751	1752
86	Robert Christie	..	..	..	..	1753	1754
87	John Bowman	..	..	..	..	1755	1756
88	Archibald Ingram	..	..	..	..	1757	1758
89	Colin Dunlop	..	..	..	..	1759	1760
90	Archibald Ingram	..	..	..	..	1761	1762
91	George Brown	..	..	..	..	1763	1764

92	Arthur Connell	..	..	..	..	..	..	1765	1766
93	John Coats Campbell	..	..	..	..	..		1767	1768
94	Archibald Smellie	..	..	..	..	..	..	1769	1770
95	George Brown	..	..	..	..	..	..	1771	1772
96	James Buchanan	..	..	..	..	..	..	1773	1774
97	John Coats Campbell		..	..	..	..		1775	1776
98	Hugh Wylie	..	..	..	..	..	..	1777	1778
99	Alexander McCaul	..	..	..	..	..		1779	1780
100	John Coats Campbell	..	..	..	..	..		1781	1782
101	James M'Grigor	..	..	..	..	..		1783	1784
102	Alexander Brown		..	..	..	..		1785	1786
103	William Coats	..	..	..	..	..		1787	1788
104	Alexander Low	..	..	..	..	..		1789	1790
105	Gilbert Hamilton	..	..	..	..	..		1791	1790
106	John Dunlop	..	..	..	..	..		1793	1792
107	John Laurie	..	..	..	..	..		1795	1794
108	Robert Finlay	..	..	..	..	..		1797	1796
109	Archibald Smith	..	..	..	..	..		1799	1808
110	John Laurie	..	..	..	..	..		1801	1800
111	Robert Carrick	..	..	..	..	..		1803	1802
112	John Laurie	..	..	..	..	..		1805	1804
113	James Black..	..	..	..	..	..		1807	1806
114	John Hamilton	..	..	..	..	..		1809	1818
115	Robert M'Nair	..	..	..	..	..		1811	
116	Daniel Mackenzie	..	..	..	..	..		1812	1813
117	John Guthrie	..	..	..	..	..		1814	1815
118	James Ewing	..	..	..	..	..		1816	1817
119	Henry Monteith	..	..	..	..	..		1818	
120	Robert Finlay	..	..	..	..	..		1819	1820
121	William Smith	..	..	..	..	..		1821	1822
122	Mungo N. Campbell	..	..	..	..	..		1823	1824
123	Robert Dalglish	..	..	..	..	..		1825	1826
124	Alexander Garden	..	..	..	..	..		1827	1828
125	Stewart Smith	..	..	..	..	..		1829	1830
126	James Ewing	..	..	..	..	..		1831	1832
127	James Hutchison	..	..	..	..	..		1833	1834
128	James Martin	..	..	..	..	..		1835	1836
129	William Brown	..	..	..	..	..		1837	1838
130	James Browne	..	..	..	..	..		1839	1840
131	William Gray	..	..	..	..	..		1841	1842
132	Hugh Cogan	..	..	..	..	..		1843	1844
133	John Leadbetter	..	..	..	..	..		1845	1846
134	James Bogle..	..	..	..	..	..		1847	1848
135	Andrew Galbraith	..	..	..	..	..		1849	1850
136	William Connal	..	..	..	..	..		1851	1852
137	James Hannan	..	..	..	..	..		1853	1854
138	Robert Baird	..	..	..	..	1855, to 7th August			1856
139	William Connal, Interim Dean	..	from 22nd to 25th August						1856
140	William Brown	..	..	..	from 9th Sept. to 7th Oct.				1856

141	John Jamieson	.. ..	1857	1858
142	Thomas Buchanan	.. ..	1859	1860
143	Sir James Lumsden	.. ..	1861	1862
144	Alexander Ronaldson	.. ..	1863	1864
145	Sir Archibald Orr Ewing, Bart.	.. ..	1865	1866
146	John Ramsay	.. ..	1867	1868
147	Sir Archibald Orr Ewing, Bart.	.. ..	1868	
148	William M'Ewen	.. ..	1869	1870
149	Alexander Ewing	.. ..	1871	1872
150	Patrick Playfair	.. ..	1873	1874
511	Sir James King, Bart	.. ..	1875	1876
152	Sir James Watson	.. ..	1877	1878
153	James Stevenson	.. .. from 8th Oct. to 20 Nov.,	1878	
154	Patrick Playfair	.. ..	1879	
155	James Buchanan Mirrlees	.. ..	1880	1881
156	Alexander Stephen	.. ..	1882	1883
157	William M'Ewen	.. ..	1884	1885
158	Walter Graham Blackie, Ph.D., LL.D.	.. .. ..	1886	1887
159	William Walls	.. ..	1888	1889
160	John Ure, LL.D.	.. ..	1890	1891
161	John Guthrie Smith	.. ..	1892	1893
162	James Reid	.. from 10th October, 1893, to 23rd June,	1894	
163	Sir James King, Bart., LL.D.	.. .. .. to 9th October	1894	
164	Hugh Brown	.. ..	1895	1896
165	Donald Graham, C.I.E.	.. ..	1897	1898
166	Sir James Bell, Bart.	.. ..	1899	1900
167	Robert Gourlay, LL.D.	.. ..	1901	1902
168	The Right Hon. George Arbuthnot, Lord Inverclyde	..	1903	1904
169	Robert King	.. ..	1905	1906
170	Sir Thomas Mason	.. ..	1907	1908
171	Matthew Pearce Campbell	.. ..	1909	1910
172	Francis Henderson	.. ..	1911	1912
173	Sir John Archibald Roxburgh, LL.D.	.. .. ..	1913	1914
174	James David Hedderwick, LL.D.	.. .. ..	1915	1916
175	Sir Hugh Reid, Bart., C.B.E., LL.D.	.. .. ..	1917	1918
176	Richard H. Hunter	.. ..	1919	1920
177	Sir Alexander Gracie, K.B.E., M.V.O.	.. .. ..	1921	1922
178	Sir Frederick C. Gardiner, K.B.E., LL.D.	.. ..	1923	1924
179	Robert T. Moore, D.Sc.	.. ..	1925	1926
180	Charles Ker, LL.D.	.. ..	1927	1928
181	Robert Robertson, LL.D.	.. ..	1929	1930
182	George W. Service	.. ..	1931	1932
183	Sir George A. Mitchell, LL.D.	.. ..	1933	1934
184	Claud A. Allan	.. ..	1935	1936
185	J. A. Ralston Mitchell	.. ..	1937	1938
186	William Cuthbert	.. ..	1939	1940
187	Sir Robert Bruce, LL.D.	.. ..	1941	1942
188	Sir A. S. Macharg	.. ..	1943	1944
189	D. Norman Sloan	.. ..	1945	1946

190	Norman MacLeod, C.M.G., D.S.O.	1947	1948
191	The Rt. Hon. John Alan, Lord Inverclyde	1949	1950
192	Sir David Allan Hay, K.B.E.	1951	1952
193	The Rt. Hon. Lord Maclay, K.B.E.	1953	1954
194	W. H. Marr	1955	1956
195	Sir Ian F. C. Bolton, Bt., K.B.E., H.M.L., LL.D. ..	1957	1958
196	H. Yates	1959	1960
197	Daniel Duncan, D.L.	1961	1962
198	J. Martin Baxter	1963	1964
199	J. W. H. Gow, C.B.E.	1965	1966
200	T. G. Robinson, O.B.E., T.D.	1967	

COLLECTORS
MERCHANTS HOUSE OF GLASGOW

1	Archibald Faulds	1605	
2	Robert Bogill	1624	
3	John Herbertson	1632	
4	John Gilmour, yr.	1633	
5	William Hyndschaw	1642	
6	Cuthbert Campbell	1650	
7	James Barnes	1656	
8	Thomas Davidson	1657	1658
9	Andrew Gibsone	1659	1660
10	John Louk	1661	1662
11	John Cauldwell	1663	
12	Peter Gemmill	1664	
13	John Corse	1665	1668
14	John Craig	1669	
15	George Herbertsone	1670	1672
16	John Stirling	1673	
17	James Biskett	1674	1675
18	George Muirhead	1676	1677
19	James Stirling	1678	1679
20	William Napier	1680	1683
21	William Anderson	1684	1685
22	James Bogle	1686	1687
23	Andrew Scott	1688	1689
24	John Ritchie	1690	1691
25	John Coats	1692	1693
26	Robert Boyd	1694	1695
27	John Anderson	1696	1697
28	Andrew Scott	1698	1699
29	John Buchanan	1700	1701
30	Robert M'Goun	1702	1704
31	James Smyth	1705	1706
32	William Gow	1707	1708
33	John Whythill	1709	1710
34	James Christie	1711	1736
35	John Riddell	1737	1749
36	William Robb	1750	1751
37	James Barrie	1752	1753
38	John Wilson	1754	1758
39	Ebenezer Monro	1759	1763
40	John Carlile	1764	1766

41	James Hill	1767	1788
42	James Hill and James Hill, jun.	1789	1790
43	James Hill	1791	1818
44	Laurence Hill, LL.D.	1819	1837
45	Robert Buntine, *Collector and Clerk*	1837	1850
46	Archibald Newall, *Collector and Clerk*	1850	1858
47	John Smith, *Collector and Clerk*	1858	1866
48	William H. Hill, LL.D., *Collector and Clerk*	1866	1912
49	James A. M'Callum, LL.D., *Collector and Clerk* ..	1912	1948
50	T. L. Grahame Reid, W.S., *Collector and Clerk* ..	1948	